CW01261909

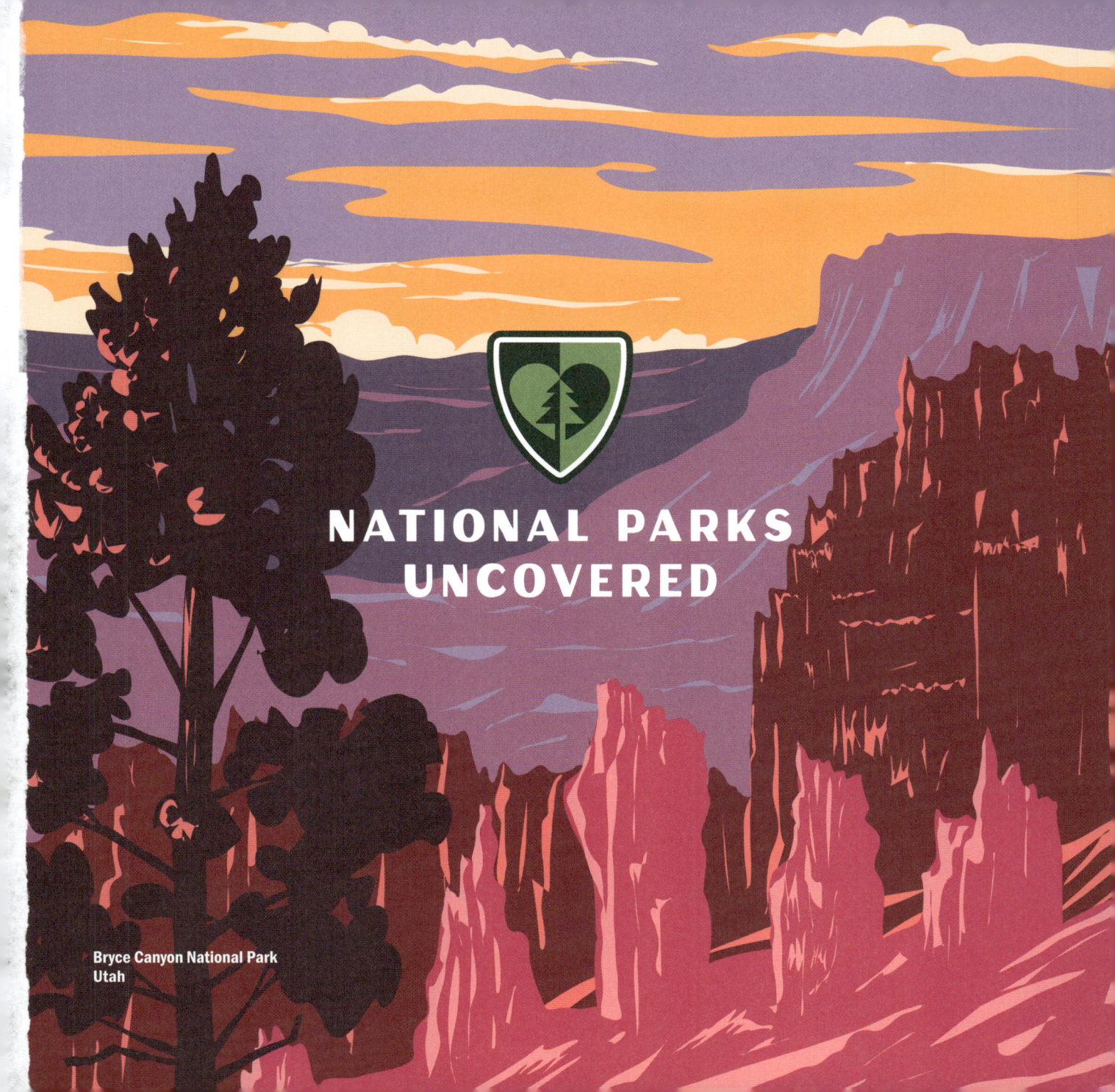

NATIONAL PARKS UNCOVERED

Bryce Canyon National Park
Utah

Glacier National Park
Montana

![logo] **National Parks**

UNCOVERED

AN EPIC RESOURCE FOR PARK LOVERS AND ANYONE OBSESSED WITH AMERICA'S BEST IDEA

LINDA MOHAMMAD

EPIC INK

Rocky Mountain National Park
Colorado

To my national-park-loving folks: the weekend warriors, the full-time adventurers, the remote workers or the retirees, the solo travelers, the dynamic duos, and the group explorers. To those who grew up being "outdoorsy" and those who never quite felt like they fit in but chose to hit the trails anyway. This book is thoughtfully curated to feed your wandering souls, to inspire your imaginations, and to indulge you to live your bucket-list life now.

To my late friend Danny Gross, the Chief Geek Ranger from the National Park Geek community, I hope you're enjoying your time with Mother Nature from up above. Thank you for the gift of the park-loving community and the life-long friendships that have blossomed from within.

To my future Junior Ranger, who has been with me through every single day of this book-writing process in utero. I cannot wait to show you America's Best Idea.

Contents

- Introduction 11
- Book Guide 14
- National Park History 16
- National Park System 101 18

The 63 National Parks 23

Pacific Northwest & Alaska 25

- Kobuk Valley National Park 26
- Gates of the Arctic National Park 28
- Denali National Park 30
- Lake Clark National Park 32
- Katmai National Park 34
- Kenai Fjords National Park 36
- Wrangell-St. Elias National Park 38
- Glacier Bay National Park 40
- North Cascades National Park 42
- Olympic National Park 44
- Mount Rainier National Park 48
- Crater Lake National Park 52

Western 57

- Redwood National Park 58
- Lassen Volcanic National Park 62
- Yosemite National Park 64
- Kings Canyon National Park 70
- Sequoia National Park 72
- Pinnacles National Park 76
- Death Valley National Park 78
- Channel Islands National Park 82
- Joshua Tree National Park 84
- Great Basin National Park 90
- Grand Canyon National Park 92
- Petrified Forest National Park 98
- Saguaro National Park 100
- Haleakalā National Park 104
- Hawai'i Volcanoes National Park 106
- National Park of American Samoa 110

Rocky Mountain 115

- Glacier National Park 116
- Yellowstone National Park 122
- Grand Teton National Park 128
- Zion National Park 132

Bryce Canyon National Park 138
Capitol Reef National Park 142
Canyonlands National Park 144
Arches National Park 146
Mesa Verde National Park 150
Black Canyon of the Gunnison National Park 152
Rocky Mountain National Park 154
Great Sand Dunes National Park 160
Theodore Roosevelt National Park 162
Wind Cave National Park 164
Badlands National Park 166

Southwest **171**
Hot Springs National Park 172
Carlsbad Caverns National Park 174
White Sands National Park 176
Big Bend National Park 180
Guadalupe Mountains National Park 182

Midwest **185**
Indiana Dunes National Park 186
Isle Royale National Park 188
Voyageurs National Park 190

    Gateway Arch National Park 192

    Cuyahoga Valley National Park 194

Southeast *201*

    Biscayne National Park.. 202

    Dry Tortugas National Park 204

    Everglades National Park... 206

    Mammoth Cave National Park... 208

    Great Smoky Mountains National Park 210

    Congaree National Park 216

    Virgin Islands National Park 218

Mid-Atlantic *221*

    Shenandoah National Park 222

    New River Gorge National Park 224

North Atlantic *229*

    Acadia National Park... 230

Beyond the 63 National Parks 236

Love Your Parks 240

Resources 244

Credits 246

Image Credits 246

Acknowledgments.. 250

About the Author 253

Rocky Mountain National Park
Colorado

Introduction

Ranging from the West Coast to the East Coast, from the Pacific Ocean all the way up to Alaska, our national parks are numerous and diverse, covering a variety of terrains and landscapes. These national treasures are protected for various natural, cultural, geological, and historical purposes, as well as "for the benefit and enjoyment of the people." Some people have it on their bucket list to visit the magnificent wonders of Yellowstone or the Grand Canyon, while some, like myself, have made it their mission to experience all 63 of the designated national parks here in the United States.

If you're like me, you don't need a specific reason to visit the national parks. But if you ever feel you have to convince your partner, friends, or family members why they should visit, there are some very compelling reasons. Each park, big or small, has a wealth of unique information to learn from, such as biodiversity in the area, geological history, and regional culture dating back to prehistoric times. When I first started my national park bucket-list journey in 2016, my motivations were exercise (via hiking), escape (through weekend trips away from work), and exploration (feeding into personal growth that later heightened my confidence, sense of wonder, and adventure meter). Whatever your reasons may be, my wish is that you always prioritize the conservation and preservation aspects of the parks during your visits.

Printed in these pages are the voices and stories of people who are passionate about our national parks. Storytelling is my forte, but as I interviewed all the contributors for the parks' love stories and travel recommendations, I was humbled to be trusted with so many cherished memories and pro tips. Since you picked up (or were gifted) this book, chances are you are also a national park lover with your own memories and stories.

Growing up in Malaysia, the most "outdoorsy" activity I did was go to a motivational camp when I was a teenager that took place in a rainforest. It was a one-and-done experience for me at the time, as I can still vividly recall a lively leech on a tree trunk, looking to hop onto its next host. My first (positive) national park memory comes from a visit to Rocky Mountain National Park in Colorado, circa 2004. It was my second year living in the United States while attending Colorado School of Mines in Golden, and several of my Malaysian friends were visiting from Wisconsin during winter break. I was stumped as to the most Colorado things to show them. Then I realized Rocky Mountain National Park is a mere 60-mile drive from Golden. I remember seeing snow, (rocky) mountains, and a herd of elk at the park.

After that first taste of the national parks, my next visit wasn't until almost five years later. I opted to pursue my masters degree in engineering at the same school and happily took a graduate class studying structural geology (because geology rocks!). We went on a weeklong field trip to study rock formations in Arches and Canyonlands National Parks, and all other red rocks in between. I loved every minute of the field trip because I got to geek out over geology and rocks, even if I wasn't much of a hiker at the time.

My bucket-list journey to experience all the designated national parks in the US started in 2016, coincidentally during the centennial anniversary of the National Park Service. At the time, there were 59 national parks in the country, and I aspired to visit them all before I turned 59 (I was 34 at the time). Living in central California, seven of the nine California national parks are within two to four hours' driving distance from me, making it an attainable goal. Within six months, I had visited all nine California national parks, along with the 19 other National Park Service sites in the state (more about the variation of park designations in the next few pages).

So, where to go next? I started adventuring to neighboring states like Utah, Washington, and Arizona, which then quickly escalated into catching flights on weekends to visit the farther parks as I made my way to the East Coast and Alaska. Before I knew it, I was approaching the end of my national park bucket-list goals (with plenty of revisits in between)—and then two more parks got redesignated, increasing the national park count to 61. Ironically, my final few parks on the list weren't the remote ones like some of the Alaska parks or National Park of American Samoa. My final three parks of the 61 were the Florida national parks, with Everglades being the last in 2019 (at least at the time, before White Sands and New River Gorge were added to the list).

Looking back at my journey experiencing America's Best Idea, I can't help but see how the experiences transformed me into the person that I am today. The parks changed me, from a timid individual who constantly second-guessed myself, my capabilities, and, at times, my worth, to becoming someone who is confident in my aptitude, secure in my self-worth, more independent than I was before, and the best one yet, the freest I have ever felt.

I hope you will find plenty of inspiration as you flip through the pages of this book and meet the people who have proudly shared their stories and experiences at our national parks. I also hope that you share your national park love with others within your circle by taking them along on your next park visit or simply by sharing this book. Make sure to share your adventures with me—I'd love to hear all about them!

Happy trails!

—Linda Mohammad,
The Bucket List Traveler
(Instagram: @thebucketlisttraveler)

Book Guide

More than just a long list of things to do or a series of "must-do" hikes, this book is a curation of some of the most meaningful personal park stories, accompanied by some never-before-seen photographs captured by park lovers across the country and other stunning images of our parks. Covering what I call the "big" 63 parks (parks officially designated as national parks), the book is divided into sections by regions of the country, west to east, with parks within that region listed north to south. If you're familiar with the Passport to Your National Parks program, which offers stamps for all 400-plus park units under the management of the National Park Service, the regional divisions in this book mimic that layout. From the Pacific Northwest and Alaska, crossing through the Rocky Mountains and Midwest to the North Atlantic, with all the other regions in between, each park possesses a unique landscape and history for us to explore.

After a short history lesson on our beloved national parks and the National Park Service as an agency, you'll see profiles on all 63 of the "big parks"—those special national parks that have captured the American imagination for generations. And don't worry, we'll also explore those 300-plus "small parks," many of which are probably closer than you think (more on them later). For the 63 national parks, each profile will include background information, personal anecdotes, treasured memories, stunning landscapes, and unique perspectives featuring the park rangers from these national parks and members of our park-loving community.

One note about the year of each park's establishment, as it can be a bit tricky. The year given first refers to when the park was initially created for protection. About half of our current national parks gained protection as different entities within the National Park Service, such as national monuments, before being redesignated later as national parks. In those cases, the national park redesignation date is in parenthesis after the establishment date, for your reference. The visitation numbers provided for every park are based on 2023 statistics.

    At the back of the book, you'll find a list of resources to help you plan your next trip to the national parks. Every experience in a national park is unique due to not just its location, but also the season in which you visit; the park's size, popularity, amenities, and accessibility; and any potential safety risks or inclement weather.

Glacier National Park
Montana

National Park History

The origin of the national park idea dates back to the 1800s, during the age of westward expansion in America. In 1872, 2.2 million acres of land were set aside in the Yellowstone region to become the world's very first national park. The founding of Yellowstone National Park sparked a worldwide national park movement. For half a century, national parks and monuments were under the supervision of the Department of the Interior (DOI), while others were supervised by the Department of War or the Department of Agriculture. Of course, the lack of a centralized federal agency dedicated to these places became an issue. Thus, the birth of the National Park Service (NPS).

The NPS mission of conservation dates back to 1916, when President Woodrow Wilson signed the Organic Act to create the agency. In 1933, an Executive Order was signed by President Franklin D. Roosevelt to transfer a number of national monuments and military sites to the care of the NPS, as well. Then, during the Progressive Era in the early twentieth century, which brought widespread social and environmental activism across the United States, there came to be two opposing factions: conservationists and preservationists. Although the two words are often used interchangeably, they represent opposite ends of the spectrum. Conservationists sought to regulate human use of natural resources, while preservationists fought to eliminate human impact altogether.

On one hand, conservation ensures humans remain connected to the outdoors not only to recreate, but also to benefit from the utilization of our natural resources. On the other hand, preservation is crucial to the protection of endangered species.

Thankfully, these philosophies of land management somehow managed to coexist, resulting in practical protection of our natural open spaces.

I would be remiss if I didn't acknowledge how conservation at the national parks affects Indigenous Peoples, who were often removed from their ancestral homelands in order to create these protected areas. For example, when Yosemite was first created in 1890, the way of life of the native Miwok people was severely restricted. In 1933, a new "Indian Village" was constructed as a way to control the native population in the park. Each time a resident lost their employment or retired from the park service, their lease would end, forcing them to leave Yosemite Valley. As a result, the Miwok's population in the park was cut in half by 1940. More than a decade later, the park service enacted a new policy where only permanent government employees could remain in the village, forcing more of the Miwok people out of the park. By 1966, the last of the Miwok park employees retired and left Yosemite Valley.

Despite this dark past of displacement, the Indigenous groups of Yosemite have continued to advocate and lobby for federal recognition and use of their ancestral lands by working with the National Park Service. In 2022, the agency issued a nationwide policy guidance to strengthen Tribal co-stewardship of national park lands and waters. Currently, the National Park Service has more than 80 co-stewardship agreements with the Indigenous tribes, four of which outline co-management of parks. As a park lover and steward myself, I encourage you to recreate responsibly and to be respectful of the land that you're recreating on. Together, we can preserve our parks and share the stories of the land and those who came before us.

National Park System 101

At the time of publication, the National Park Service manages over 400 individual park units covering more than 85 million acres in all 50 states, the District of Columbia, Puerto Rico, the US Virgin Islands, Guam, and American Samoa. The diversity of these parks is reflected in the variety of designations available. While there are at least 19 naming designations, these units are commonly referred to as simply "parks." There are two overarching themes: natural values and importance in history. Below is a breakdown of the nuances between the different designations.

Natural Values

Parks under this header consist of areas that have one or more distinctive attributes, such as forest, grassland, tundra, desert, estuary, or river systems. They are protected for their natural values and may offer windows on the past through geological history; feature imposing landforms like mountains, mesas, thermal areas, or caverns; and may also be habitats of abundant or rare flora and fauna.

🌲 **NATIONAL PARKS** generally contain a variety of resources and encompass large land or water areas to help provide adequate protection of the resources within its bounds. They can only be created by an act of Congress, and the taking or consumption of natural resources from these lands is prohibited. All 63 national parks showcased in this book fall under this designation (my personal favorite is Petrified Forest National Park).

🌲 **NATIONAL MONUMENTS** are intended to preserve at least one nationally significant resource. They're usually smaller than national parks and have less diversity of attractions. The Antiquities Act of 1906 authorized the president to declare by public proclamation landmarks, structures, and other objects of historic or scientific interest situated on lands owned or controlled by the government to be national monuments. Chiricahua National Monument in Arizona is a perfect example of a national monument, though I personally feel it deserves national park status.

🌲 **NATIONAL PRESERVES** are established primarily for the protection of certain resources. Activities like hunting and fishing or the extraction of minerals and fuels may be permitted if such activities do not jeopardize the natural values. A personal favorite of mine is the Mojave National Preserve in California, which protects the largest and densest Joshua tree population in the world!

🌲 **NATIONAL LAKESHORES and NATIONAL SEASHORES** focus on the preservation of natural values along shoreline areas and also provide water-oriented recreation. For example, Point Reyes National Seashore in California preserves 80-plus miles of shoreline, including dozens of miles of sand beaches, making it a great spot for whale watching during migration season.

🌲 **NATIONAL RIVERS** preserve free-flowing streams and their immediate environment as long as they feature at least one remarkable natural, cultural, or recreational value. They also provide opportunities for outdoor activities like hiking, canoeing, and hunting. America's First National River runs through Arkansas, where the Buffalo National River flows freely for 135 miles.

🌲 **NATIONAL SCENIC TRAILS** are generally long-distance footpaths winding through areas of natural beauty. A popular example is the Appalachian Trail, which crosses 13 states over its 2,190 miles.

🌲 **NATIONAL HISTORIC TRAILS** recognize original trails or routes of travel of national historical significance. The Trail of Tears crosses nine states over its 5,045 miles, commemorating the survival of Cherokee people that were forcibly removed from their homelands. Another moving example is the Selma to Montgomery National Historic Trail in Alabama.

Importance in History

These park units preserve places and commemorate persons, events, and activities important in the nation's history, ranging from archeological sites associated with prehistoric Indigenous People's civilizations to sites related to the lives of modern Americans. The spaces under this heading are customarily preserved or restored to reflect their appearance during the period of their greatest historical significance.

🌲 **NATIONAL HISTORIC SITES** usually contain a single historical feature that was directly associated with its subject. Derived from the Historic Sites Act of 1935, a number of historic sites were established by Secretaries of the Interior, but most have been authorized by acts of Congress. Two impactful examples for me are the Washita Battlefield and Manzanar National Historic Sites.

🌲 **NATIONAL HISTORICAL PARKS** cover greater physical areas and complexity than the previous sites. Independence National Historical Park in Pennsylvania is a popular example, preserving several sites associated with the American Revolution and the nation's founding.

🌲 **NATIONAL MILITARY PARKS, NATIONAL BATTLEFIELD PARKS, NATIONAL BATTLEFIELD SITES, and NATIONAL BATTLEFIELDS** are all areas associated with American military history where notable battles were fought in the United States, ranging from attacks on Indigenous People to events of the Civil War. I particularly enjoyed my visit to Shiloh National Military Park in Tennessee, as it is the namesake ship where my husband spent several years of his active-duty navy days.

Mount Rushmore National Memorial
South Dakota

🌲 **NATIONAL MEMORIALS** are primarily commemorative. They do not need to be sites or structures historically associated with their subjects. Two famous examples of these are the Mount Rushmore and Pearl Harbor National Memorials.

🌲 **NATIONAL RECREATION AREAS** were originally designated surrounding large reservoirs, emphasizing water-based recreation, but have now evolved to include areas near major population centers. They combine scarce open spaces with the preservation of significant historic resources and important natural areas to provide outdoor recreation for large numbers of people. An unexpected example of this designation is the Golden Gate National Recreation Area in California, encompassing areas on both sides of the Golden Gate Bridge and the bridge itself.

🌲 **NATIONAL PARKWAYS** are designed for slow travel, offering opportunities to drive through areas of scenic interest. They're intended for scenic motoring along a protected corridor and often connect cultural sites. Driving the entirety of Blue Ridge Parkway during peak fall colors is still on my bucket list.

🌲 **PARKS and GARDENS** account for 11 parks covering a variety of topics, including Wolf Trap National Park for the Performing Arts in Virginia.

Grand Canyon National Park
Arizona

The 63 National Parks

Kenai Fjords National Park
Alaska

Pacific Northwest & Alaska

The Pacific Northwest and Alaska region is home to a number of volcanoes that stretch from northern Oregon all the way north to the Last Frontier. In this region, you'll hear stories and recommendations from park rangers based in Alaska, Oregon, and Washington State, along with park lovers and outdoorspeople who found beauty and charm in landscapes of fire and ice. The superlatives here occur in some of the most unique environments in North America, like the largest active sand dune field in the Arctic, the tallest waterfall in the continental United States, and the deepest lake in the nation.

Pacific Northwest & Alaska

Kobuk Valley National Park

Land of the caribou and home to the largest active dune field in arctic North America, Kobuk Valley National Park ranked in the top three of the least-visited and most remote national parks in the United States. There are no roads to access the park, so most visitors fly in from Kotzebue or Bettles on authorized air taxis. Although Kobuk Valley is hard to get to, the experience once you're there is worth it.

Ranger Jonathan Nicholson got his first taste of working in a national park after graduating college and serving in the army for four years. He had some time before starting his graduate school, so he decided to become an adult leader for the Youth Conservation Corp, supervising high school kids in Yellowstone National Park. "That was the hook," he says. "Not only the landscape and a park like Yellowstone, but it's also about the program. When you couple them together, that was enough to set the hook into me. Once I did my master's, I pivoted again, and instead of pursuing going into the classroom and being a teacher, I started looking for education and interpretation jobs in the National Park Service."

Kobuk Valley is remote, but that's part of what makes it special. "You have this massive sand dune field that sits above the Arctic Circle, and that in itself is unique," Ranger Jon says. "But you also have the

Meandering rivers create stunning curved patterns visible from the air.

ESTABLISHED	LOCATION
1978 (redesignated 1980)	Northwestern Alaska

SIZE	VISITATION NO.
2,736 square miles	17,616

LAND ACKNOWLEDGMENT
Ancestral land of the Iñupiaq and Koyukon Athabaskan people

FOR MORE INFO, VISIT:
www.nps.gov/kova

Expansive views await as you land by the Kobuk River bank.

beautiful valley that is the majority of the 1.9 million acres of national park land that is Kobuk Valley. So all the resources, whether that's the Kobuk River or the different mountain ranges like the Baird Mountains, it's just a really unique park and some of that uniqueness is due to its remoteness and how hard it is to get to."

TRAILBLAZING!

Some of North America's very first inhabitants (both humans and animals) have called Kobuk Valley home. **Woolly mammoths** roamed the area during the last ice age, and **caribou herds** have been making their annual migration across the river for thousands of years.

To start the planning process for your visit to Kobuk Valley, Ranger Jon suggested that you start with the park's list of authorized air taxis, found on the park website, since the outfitters have a wealth of knowledge that can help you craft the experience you're looking for. "Do your research ahead of time, be prepared for the different conditions that your trip might be, whether a scenic flight with brief stop in Kobuk Valley or a multi-day, multi-week expedition down the Kobuk River packrafting one of the side drainages," he says. "You're going to encounter a lot of different weather conditions depending on the time of year. And lastly, remain flexible. Traveling in Alaska is challenging. The weather can be fickle and shift, and that can really ruin your plan. So having patience and the ability to work through some of those situations and come up with options, it would help if you have prepared for the second, third, or fourth option."

Pacific Northwest & Alaska

Gates of the Arctic National Park

ESTABLISHED	LOCATION
1978 (redesignated 1980)	Northern Alaska
SIZE	**VISITATION NO.**
13,238 square miles	11,045
LAND ACKNOWLEDGMENT	
Ancestral land of the Nunamiut Inupiat and Koyukon Athabaskan people	
FOR MORE INFO, VISIT:	
www.nps.gov/gaar	

As the name might suggest, this park is the northernmost national park in the United States, with one of the access points sitting roughly 60 miles north of the Arctic Circle. With no trails, no established campsites, and no roads leading into Gates of the Arctic National Park, the vastness of the area provides a solid amount of solitude for the adventurous at heart.

Ranger Eric Tidwell didn't know much about Gates of the Arctic in his senior year of college, but he did know he was ready for an adventure. He interned at Gates of the Arctic and Pinnacles National Parks two summers in a row via the Student Conservation Association before landing a permanent position as park ranger

Rugged peaks, wild scenic rivers, and vast landscapes fill this road-less park.

almost a decade ago. "The best part about my job is learning something new every day," he says. "You are constantly putting on different hats, working each new problem as it comes up, often with limited resources, often in a backcountry setting. There is always a puzzle to be solved, and it is constantly rewarding to see your progress benefit these special places."

The question that he often gets asked as a ranger at Gates of the Arctic is "How do I get there?" Admittedly, the park requires detailed logistical planning. "My favorite part about this park is its remoteness. As the float plane takes off after dropping you on a remote lake, and your ears fill with the silence of the landscape, you'll begin to understand what I mean," Ranger Eric says. "This is as true of wilderness as you will find anywhere. Because of this, coupled with the difficult terrain, Gates of the Arctic is not the place to try hiking for the first time. We often say that an experienced hiker used to going 20 to 30 miles in a day, can expect to travel 6 miles a day in the park."

"Due to the park being a roadless wilderness, chartering a flight is a popular form of travel. After doing research and getting an idea of what you may want to accomplish in the park, talk to a flight operator and see where they can land and what their expectations and limitations are for flying. This will begin to narrow the scope of what is feasible for your group."

Float down the pristine rivers and experience the solitude and isolation of Gates of the Arctic's wilderness.

In a park as big as Gates of the Arctic, it's hard to pick a favorite spot or make just one recommendation. As Ranger Eric says, it would take multiple lifetimes to explore. But, he says, "A favorite thing to do in the park would be to float one of the six wild and scenic rivers. This form of non-motorized boat travel allows you to cover many more miles in a day than you would be able to otherwise, and with the size of the landscape and the fly-in nature of the park, it often makes the most sense. As you adventure, you may come across cultural or subsistence practices occurring within the park. Many visitors don't realize that this land is still actively used by Alaska Natives, as it has been for more than 10,000 years. For them, it is home. Please show respect to any animals, structures, or other people you may come across."

TRAILBLAZING!

Gates of the Arctic has six designated wild rivers within its boundaries which have served as byways for wildlife and humans alike for centuries. **Aufeis** (overflow ice) is common in the northern rivers and can be up to 15 feet thick.

Pacific Northwest & Alaska

Denali National Park

ESTABLISHED	LOCATION
1917	Central Alaska
SIZE	**VISITATION NO.**
7,408 square miles	498,722

LAND ACKNOWLEDGMENT
Ancestral land of the Ahtna, Dena'ina, Koyukon, Upper Kuskokwim, and Tanana peoples

FOR MORE INFO, VISIT:
www.nps.gov/dena

Denali National Park is home to North America's tallest peak, which is pretty impressive. But being home to the only working sled-dog kennel in a national park is also something to brag about. Sled dogs have been a significant part of the Alaskan landscape for hundreds of years. Within the park itself, teams of sled dogs help park rangers access and monitor the park's ground during wintertime in areas that are only accessible by foot, dog sledding, or air.

Ranger James Seale's earliest memory of visiting a national park is visiting the Rocky Mountains when he was a teenager. For someone who grew up in Florida, surrounded by alligators and swamp land, being amongst the towering mountains was a breath of fresh air. "My journey to becoming a park ranger here in Alaska was unusual and not where I was expecting my life to take me," he admits. "After spending two summers in Alaska working in the Kenai Peninsula with a vacation rental company, I was searching for potential winter jobs. I found a listing for a park ranger position in Denali National Park and Preserve as a 'kennel ranger,' working with and exploring Denali National Park's wilderness with a team of 30 freight-hauling-style Alaskan Huskies. My imagination lit up and I could just see myself adventuring and braving the cold. So I called, emailed, interviewed, and finally at the end of it all . . . got rejected! Long story short, I was called back a few days later and the park offered the position to me."

Besides his human coworkers, Ranger James's favorite parts of his job as a kennel ranger are his canine colleagues. "Alaska has charmed me in every

The tall mountain creates its own weather, so it's only visible around thirty percent of the time.

way imaginable and I couldn't imagine my life anywhere else now. I get to protect natural, historic, and cultural resources while inspiring others to do so as well. I'm not sure I could ever find a job that's more rewarding for me personally than the one I have now," he says. "The dogs and people I work with every day are truly some of the most extraordinary beings on this planet and I am beyond grateful for each and every one of them."

To find adventures in Denali, Ranger James recommends forging your own path: "Wilderness is as accessible as you make it. Laying in the grass observing a snail meandering around a flower is just as wild and beautiful as a 1,400-pound moose meandering around a spruce tree." When he's not hanging out with the canine rangers, Ranger James can be found wandering the ridgeline in the park. In the summer, park rangers offer daily demonstrations of the sled dogs, a unique experience only to be had at Denali National Park.

For photographer and national park enthusiast Mick Dees, backpacking in Denali during fall was a trip

Vibrant fall colors on display amongst the trees and tundra shrubs of Denali National Park.

TRAILBLAZING!

There are an estimated **600 low magnitude seismic events** per year within the Denali National Park boundaries due to shifting tectonic plates in the area.

to remember. "Up here in Alaska, the entire mountain sides and valleys are transformed into all the colors of the rainbow once the taiga and tundra start changing. So, getting off-trail and backpacking within those colors, glaciers in the background, following rivers, and keeping a close eye out for grizzly bears and rutting bull moose, it's a truly wild and epic adventure," he explains. "This past backpacking trip, I came across two grizzlies, five bull moose, and a white wolf!"

Pacific Northwest & Alaska

Lake Clark National Park

ESTABLISHED	**LOCATION**
1978 (redesignated 1980)	Southwest Alaska
SIZE	**VISITATION NO.**
4,093 square miles	16,728
LAND ACKNOWLEDGMENT	
Ancestral land of the Dena'ina people	
FOR MORE INFO, VISIT:	
www.nps.gov/lacl	

Initially created to safeguard the watershed that plays a significant role in protecting the red salmon fishery in Bristol Bay, Lake Clark National Park preserves some of Alaska's finest landscapes, including an array of mountains, thundering waterfalls, and turquoise lakes fed by glacial streams. Like its neighbor Katmai, in Lake Clark you'll find excellent bear viewing, as they feed on salmon and clams along the coastline.

Growing up frequenting a family cabin surrounded by national forests, Ranger Chelsea Niles's relationship with public lands was predominantly utilitarian, somewhere she gathered firewood for the cabin's fire pit. Then, while road-tripping from Michigan to California for an internship to study marine biology one summer, she took a detour to Yellowstone National Park for the first time.

"This detour and place changed the course of my life and gave me new purpose," she says. "I left Yellowstone and the Greater Yellowstone Ecosystem full of wonder, curiosity, and memories of the most incredible place I had ever been. After several days and many miles between me and Yellowstone, I made it to my internship location and knew that I wanted to be a part of protecting our

Lake Clark's coastal brown bears can be found on the estuaries near Cook Inlet, where the flowing rivers are filled with salmon and the tidal flats brim with clams.

nation's national park sites forever. When I returned to college after my internship, I changed my focus to public lands stewardship and never looked back."

Besides rocking the cool flat hat as part of the park ranger uniform, Ranger Chelsea loves watching people falling in love with their public lands. "To be able to facilitate deep connections between people and places is pure magic," she says. "My favorite part about Lake Clark is its relevance to people who may never visit, as well as the access and opportunity that comes with innovation. This is a place where we get to think outside the box and be innovative in the effort of equity and inclusion."

The park can only be accessed by small plane or boat, making visitations more costly and tougher logistically—but, if it's possible for you to visit, it is more than worth it. "For some, Lake Clark's two prominent volcanoes are the scene they capture in a picture. For others, it's the backdrop of the place they call home. As an interpreter, I see this as an incredible opportunity to facilitate connection between Lake Clark and the people who may have seen it their entire lives from afar without realizing it," Ranger Chelsea explains. "People protect what they love. Unbeknownst to many, people love this park through its viewshed. By recognizing the park has relevance and significance outside its mapped borders, we are presented with an invaluable opportunity to use our platform and reach to tell important stories to more people than we could ever serve in the park. Lake Clark is special. It's wild, it's beautiful, it's a people's wilderness, and it's a place for everyone."

The dynamic forces of volcanoes and glaciers still actively shape the rugged peaks we see in the park today.

TRAILBLAZING!

Indigenous People of the area call this area **Qizhjeh Vena**, meaning "place people gather lake" in the Dena'ina language. Subsistence—the practice of hunting, fishing, and gathering—is still practiced by the Dena'ina people today.

Pacific Northwest & Alaska

Katmai National Park

ESTABLISHED	LOCATION
1918 (redesignated 1980)	Southern Alaska

SIZE	VISITATION NO.
5,741 square miles	33,763

LAND ACKNOWLEDGMENT
Ancestral land of the Alutiiq (Sugpiaq), Inuit, Yupik and Dena'ina Athabaskan people

FOR MORE INFO, VISIT:
www.nps.gov/katm

The geological landscape at Katmai National Park, created by the Novarupta Volcano a little over a century ago, is stunning, but that's not why this park is on the bucket list for many national park goers and wildlife lovers. Home to North America's largest protected population of brown bears, visitors come to see the famous residents of the park at Brooks Falls during salmon season (typically mid-June to July, temperature dependent).

Having previously worked in Alaska at the Tongass National Forest, Matt Johnson recently moved to Katmai National Park from a smaller park in Colorado. He loves Alaska's enormous, intact ecosystems, which are "ancient, complex, and full of different and surprising lifeforms."

The only thing he loves more is the very first national park he ever visited: Bruce Peninsula National Park in Canada. "I was captivated by the clean and refreshing water that extends to the horizon for as far as I can see, the fragrance of the forest of white cedar, birch, maple, balsam fir, and white pine, the serenity of sounds of the waves upon Georgian Bay, the eerie songs of loons, and the wind sweeping over the forest," he explains. "I knew from the experience that

Katmai offers spectacular opportunities for brown bear viewing, at Brooks Falls or along the Brooks River.

> ## TRAILBLAZING!
>
> During the eruption of the **Novarupta and Mount Katmai volcanoes** in 1912, ash settled 300 feet deep in a nearby valley and the summit of Mount Katmai collapsed into a caldera. Once the valley deposits cooled, steam from fissures and fumaroles were emitted, creating the Valley of Ten Thousand Smokes.

I needed to be a park ranger when I grew up, and that I craved places like this."

Ranger Matt enjoys seeing visitors experience the awe and charm of the national parks. "Sharing this radiance with others makes me feel so good. It was what I was meant to do," he shares. "As a child, I drew a picture of me as a park ranger and I am so happy I realized this dream for myself. To me, the national parks are the pinnacles of resource conservation, enjoyment, inspiration, and human and wildlife well-being. They are America's best idea for sure. I seek national parks when I travel around the world."

If watching the brown bears at Brooks Falls is on your bucket list, there are several ways to make it happen. Many visitors opt for a day trip to Katmai via float plane, departing from Anchorage, Homer, or King Salmon in Alaska, to keep the logistics simpler. For those looking for a multi-day experience, your best bet is to either reserve a camping permit for Brooks Camp or secure a cabin at Brooks Lodge (via a lottery system two years in advance).

Personally, I decided to check off two Alaska national parks in one trip by booking an overnight trip to Lake Clark National Park and making a day trip to Katmai from there. Not only was I able to witness the salmon run at Brooks Falls, I also did a flightseeing trip the next day to take in the aerial view of the Valley of Ten Thousand Smokes. Ranger Matt also suggests a hike in the valley for an "off the beaten path" experience, either through a ranger-guided day tour or on a backcountry hike for experienced hikers.

The Valley of Ten Thousand Smokes was formed during the 1912 Novarupta-Katmai eruption.

Pacific Northwest & Alaska

Kenai Fjords National Park

Dramatic glacial landscapes are found at Spire Cove in Resurrection Bay.

Roughly two hours' drive from Anchorage is Kenai Fjords National Park, perhaps one of the two most accessible national parks in Alaska (after Denali). The drive along Seward Highway, parallel to the dramatic shoreline of Turnagain Arm, is one of the most scenic routes you'll find behind the wheel.

One of the unique aspects of the Kenai Fjords is how the different parts of the park govern your activities. On the land side, the hikes to Exit Glacier or on top of Harding Icefield are the popular choices. On the sea side, you can explore the fjords and witness the scale of the tidewater glacier via a narrated boat tour. Both national park lovers Patrick Rodden and Mick Dees have gone the adventurous route by going ice climbing.

Patrick Rodden is on a mission to see all 63 national parks in the United States, and traveling to Kenai Fjords turned out to be one of his greatest adventures in a long time. "During my visit, I pushed my limits far beyond my comfort level," he admits. "When I take trips to national parks that are far off from California, I usually go with my friend Pradeep. On this trip, we did just about everything possible that local outfitters offered to do within the park boundaries. Prior to the trip, I booked a paddle-boarding excursion amidst icebergs in the lagoon of Bear Glacier. This then expanded into a boat tour of Resurrection Bay, and hiking and ice climbing on Exit Glacier with Exit Glacier Guides."

Mick Dees now lives in Seward, Alaska, a stone's throw from Kenai Fjords. According to Mick, this park is

ESTABLISHED	LOCATION
1978 (redesignated 1980)	Southcentral Alaska
SIZE	VISITATION NO.
1,047 square miles	387,525
LAND ACKNOWLEDGMENT	
Ancestral land of the Alutiiq (Sugpiaq) people	
FOR MORE INFO, VISIT:	
www.nps.gov/kefj	

perfect for those looking to cross off some bucket-list items. "Kayaking between huge icebergs through the prettiest blue waters you'll ever see with the sound of glaciers caving in the background, whales and puffins nearby . . . this is the place for you. I know I'll never get tired of it," he says. "Adding to the epicness, I have ice-climbed within the crevasses of Exit Glacier. Hiking out on a massive glacier and dropping down into a narrow blue abyss isn't for the faint of heart, but it will be embedded in your memory forever."

A friend and I took a trip to Alaska not so long ago. Like many who visit, she was seeking adventure and had been longing to experience Alaska's glory. We took a train trip from Anchorage to Seward before hopping on a six-hour boat tour to see the tidewater glaciers in Kenai Fjords. Since it was my second time doing the boat trip, I knew what to expect. However, the boat ride was rough that day. I remember glancing at my friend and she looked as if she was about to puke! Despite the cold weather, we decided to move out to the back of the boat, which was open-air. Thankfully, she recovered just in time to see the Aialik Glacier.

The train ride to Seward is my favorite to this day. Some of the views along the tracks are available only to train passengers, since there are no roads parallel to the track in some sections.

One of five tidewater glaciers that flow from the Harding Icefield and terminate in the ocean.

TRAILBLAZING!

Fifty percent of this park is covered by ice! Kenai Fjords is also home to one-quarter of Alaska's glaciers. The longest, **Bear Glacier**, flows from the Harding Icefield and terminates in Bear Lagoon.

Pacific Northwest & Alaska

Wrangell–St. Elias National Park

One of the few national parks in Alaska that is accessible by road, Wrangell-St. Elias National Park contains some of the largest volcanoes and the greatest concentration of glaciers in North America. Rising from the ocean in Yakutat Bay all the way up to the 18,008-foot summit of Mount St. Elias, this national park is America's largest. It protects vast amounts of habitat, from temperate rainforest to tundra environments, making it a perfect home to sustain a diverse species of animals.

Ranger Jamie Hart has always been interested in nature. She grew up in the rural countryside of Illinois and spent time running through creeks, fields, and forests, then, "When it was time to go to college, I was undecided but quickly learned about forestry. I received my Bachelor of Science in forestry, specializing in outdoor recreation resource management," she says. "After completing my undergraduate degree, I decided to get further education through an online program that was built with students who worked for the National Park Service. The first two years of this degree program were just the NPS students. In the third year of the program, I attended the university in person and benefited from having peers who worked for national parks around the country. I spent a summer working as an Interpretive Park Ranger at Glacier National Park in Montana. Five seasons later, it was life-changing. I then applied for a position at Wrangell-St. Elias National Park and Preserve

An Alaskan sunset over glacier-filled valleys and endless forests.

ESTABLISHED	LOCATION
1978 (redesignated 1980)	Southcentral Alaska

SIZE	VISITATION NO.
20,587 square miles	78,305

LAND ACKNOWLEDGMENT
Ancestral land of the Ahtna, Upper Tanana, Eyak, and Tlingit people

FOR MORE INFO, VISIT:
www.nps.gov/wrst

and got it! I moved to Alaska and have stayed ever since as a Supervisory Park Ranger in Interpretation."

Her favorite part of the park is the combination of glaciers and rivers. "The glaciers feed our big, broad, braiding rivers, which allows for awesome paddling experiences. I've enjoyed packrafting on the park's rivers and creeks! [The park is] so big and takes a long time to see . . . My recommendation is to book a flightseeing tour or a backcountry drop-off. It allows you to see the park from the air, which is one of its best features. You'll get to see valley glaciers, braided rivers, hopefully wildlife, and amazing views."

My experience at Wrangell-St. Elias National Park is almost to a tee what Ranger Jamie recommends, minus the backcountry drop-off. I spent three days and two nights at the park, based in McCarthy. It's about a half-mile walk to reach the Kennecott River Pedestrian Bridge to get into the park, but staying at the McCarthy Bed and Breakfast helped keep my accommodation cost low compared to lodging options inside the park. On my first day there, I went on a private packraft trip with a guide, my first time trying the popular local activity. Packrafting is similar to kayaking, but done on a portable, lightweight, inflatable boat. The next day, I decided to brave the ice and went on a group hike atop Root Glacier. I'll admit, it's a one and done for me because I'm not a big fan of strapping crampons to my boots and walking on ice. The hike lasted almost five hours and it felt like a lifetime to me! I decided to reward my bravery by capping off my trip with a last-minute "Mile-High Cliff" flightseeing tour, which was worth the splurge.

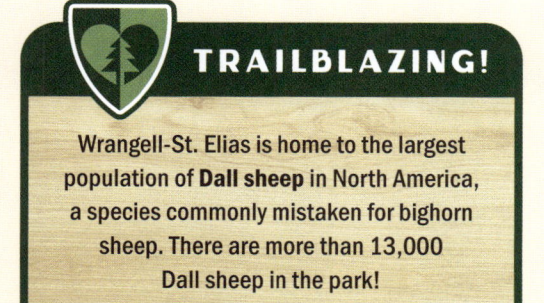

Explore the heart of Wrangell-St. Elias National Park by foot on the Root Glacier.

TRAILBLAZING!

Wrangell-St. Elias is home to the largest population of **Dall sheep** in North America, a species commonly mistaken for bighorn sheep. There are more than 13,000 Dall sheep in the park!

Pacific Northwest & Alaska

Glacier Bay National Park

ESTABLISHED	LOCATION
1925 (redesignated 1980)	Southeast Alaska
SIZE	**VISITATION NO.**
5,131 square miles	703,659
LAND ACKNOWLEDGMENT	
Ancestral land of the Huna Tlingit people	
FOR MORE INFO, VISIT:	
www.nps.gov/glba	

Best seen from the water by boat, Glacier Bay accumulates the inflow of retreating glaciers from the surrounding mountain area, filling in a 65-mile-long (and counting) fjord. Its main feature is the massive tidewater glaciers at the northern end of the fjord. Many visitors opt to arrive via a multi-day Alaskan cruise, but others, like myself, who wish to also explore the land section of Glacier Bay National Park, can fly into Juneau then take the 15-minute flight to Gustavus for a longer stay in the park.

Rugged mountain ranges, a maze of ice-scoured fjords, and glacial-carved valleys await those who venture out to Glacier Bay.

I first met Karley Nugent during a visit to Yellowstone National Park. She was working with the park's concessionaire and we both attended a meetup hosted by a Yellowstone park ranger. We hit it off, then we reconnected at Yellowstone two years later. This time around, Karley's role had changed: she was a park ranger. I was thrilled when I found out she had landed a seasonal role at Glacier Bay in the summer of 2023. Today, Ranger Karley is a permanent ranger at the Horseshoe Bend National Military Park in Alabama, but she still carries fond memories of Alaska.

"Glacier Bay was one of the most humbling places I've ever had the extraordinary experience of visiting," she says. "Like all land, Glacier Bay is sacred, and it's a place where you can truly feel the power of the Earth and the weight of its importance. What I valued most about my time there was the opportunity to work with some of the best people I've ever known, and to become a small part of a chapter of continued growth and healing between the National Park Service and the Xunaa Tlingit,

Over a quarter of this park is covered in ice.

> ### TRAILBLAZING!
> The **Huna Tlingit people** call this place **S'e Shuyee**, meaning "edge of the glacial silt." Until about 300 years ago, the Tlingit lived in the lower section of the bay before being forced out by the advancing glacier.

the co-steward of the homeland. Becoming a part of the history of these places and sharing these stories with the visitors from all over is such a joy."

Ranger Karley often reminds future visitors that Glacier Bay is truly remote and not accessible by land. "Much like all of Southeast Alaska, I have come to find, the park is a place of 'charms and challenges,'" she shares. "You have the opportunity to see and experience things not many people will get to, and the true adventure that can be found is unparalleled, in my opinion. Because of that, remember that your Glacier Bay experience is completely your own. We all have seen pictures of whales breaching, or videos of giant spires of ice falling off the tidewater glaciers and crashing into the sea. This leads people to often set high expectations for their trip into Glacier Bay. By all means, I believe that no matter what, Glacier Bay exceeds expectations! Every day is different in Glacier Bay. It's a place of constant motion, changing second by second. Embrace the fact that your time in the park is uniquely your own, and that's what makes each and every visit to Glacier Bay truly exceptional."

Ranger Karley's favorite items for the boat trips are her binoculars and camera. "Almost all my special wildlife sightings, like the bears, wolves, whale spouts, or puffins, always felt so far away from me, so having those lenses really brought me closer," she explains. "Telephoto lenses or high-powered zoom cameras are also a must-have if you're hoping to capture those memories and keep them beyond the moment."

Tidewater glaciers will break off or calve into saltwater at sea level.

Pacific Northwest & Alaska

North Cascades National Park

ESTABLISHED	LOCATION
1968	North Washington
SIZE	VISITATION NO.
789 square miles	40,351
LAND ACKNOWLEDGMENT	
Ancestral land of the Upper Skagit, Chilliwack, Lower Thompson, and Chelan people	
FOR MORE INFO, VISIT:	
www.nps.gov/noca	

Part of the Cascade Range that spreads across Northern California and up to the southern parts of British Columbia, North Cascades National Park is home to over 300 glaciers, craggy peaks, U-shaped valleys, and myriad waterfalls. The park itself is part of the larger North Cascades National Park Service Complex, which also includes Ross Lake and Lake Chelan National Recreation Areas. Despite its proximity to major cities like Seattle, North Cascades remains one of the underrated and least-visited national parks of the big 63.

Ranger Yeva Cifor didn't grow up in a family that did the classic national park road trips for vacation. In fact, she grew up in San Francisco and went to a high school located within the Golden Gate National Recreation Area without knowing it was a National Park Service site.

"After graduating college and studying agricultural science, I worked on an organic vegetable farm in the local area. I enjoyed the job, but it was physically challenging and after two summers I was feeling like I needed a change," she says. "I talked to my best friend's mom, who had been a park ranger for her career, and thought that sounded like a good job to try. I searched for opportunities in national parks and got a three-month position as a volunteer interpretive ranger at Crater Lake National Park in late winter. I was hooked!"

Now a ranger at North Cascades, she enjoys sharing her passion for the outdoors with others and

Jagged peaks, panoramic views, and alpine lakes dominate the landscape at North Cascades National Park.

connecting with visitors and hearing their stories. "I chose to work in national parks because of the diversity of parks within the National Park Service and the opportunities available to work as an interpretive park ranger," she shares. "My favorite part of North Cascades is the wide array of recreational opportunities that exist in and around this park, activities like hiking, camping, mountaineering, skiing, paddling, rafting, and fishing, just to name a few. The gorgeous scenery of mountain peaks, glaciers, and the variety of flora and fauna throughout the ecosystem make it pretty amazing as well!"

The Stephen Mather Wilderness Area is a part of the North Cascade Complex that boasts some land not accessible by car, which makes for an adventurous outing. Ranger Yeva suggests planning ahead and using the parks' website so you can experience some of her favorite trails, like Trail of the Cedars, Happy Creek Nature, Thornton Lakes, and the popular Cascade Pass and Sahale Arm Trail. She also shares, "My favorite views that are easily accessible are of the Picket Range from the Sterling Munro Boardwalk, Diablo Lake from the Diablo Lake Overlook, and Gorge Creek Falls Overlook, where you get views of the waterfall and of Gorge Lake."

Stroll the temperate rainforest trails for a taste of the diverse Pacific Northwest ecosystems.

TRAILBLAZING!

The complex **mountain-building process** in this park formed a series of what seem to be endless peaks with deep valleys carved by glaciers, which makes the mountains appear taller than they are.

Pacific Northwest & Alaska

Olympic National Park

Olympic's beauty, defined by lusciously green temperate rainforest, is unmatched. This park ranges from the edge of the Pacific Ocean all the way up to Hurricane Ridge, which is often covered in snow during the winter. Almost every story I've heard from Olympic National Park lovers and rangers alike includes exploring this park on a rainy day, which is to be expected when in the Pacific Northwest.

Ranger Amos Almy started his career as seasonal park ranger in Wrangell-St. Elias National Park after

ESTABLISHED	LOCATION
1909 (redesignated 1938)	Coastal Washington
SIZE	**VISITATION NO.**
1,442 square miles	2,947,503
LAND ACKNOWLEDGMENT	Ancestral land of the Hoh, Jamestown S'Klallam, Elwha Klallam, Makah, Port Gamble S'Klallam, Quileute, Quinault, and Skokomish people
FOR MORE INFO, VISIT:	www.nps.gov/olym

Hurricane Ridge earned its name from the wind gusts there, which reach over 75 miles per hour.

finishing his degree in environmental studies. He bopped between the other two Washington national parks before finally landing at Olympic. "My passion for the outdoors began when I was a kid growing up in Maine," he says. "I would spend summers hiking, backpacking, and canoeing all over the state. At the time, it was just a fun thing to do between school years, but in my final years in college I realized I am most comfortable outdoors and in nature. My body enjoys being outdoors and my mind enjoys nature as well. I'm fortunate to be able to work in a field that I am so passionate about."

Ranger Molly Pittman, on the other hand, never attended ranger programs when she visited National Park Service sites in her younger years, but her family still valued wilderness, exploration, and storytelling. "When I realized I could combine these into a career, it felt unreal," she says. "I credit my National Park Service career to one particularly inspiring interpreter in Grand Teton National Park, Elizabeth Maki. Rangers are constantly learning and sharing knowledge. It's the ultimate nerd job."

For Ranger Molly, the best feature of Olympic National Park is its diversity. "Over 95 percent of the park is designated wilderness that stretches from the snowy summits to the sea. You can climb in the alpine, stroll beneath moss-blanketed trees, and explore tidepools along the coast. We have some of the quietest places in the country. But even when you're surrounded by the park's sounds, you can't help but feel at ease. The rivers, moss, and mountains clear the mind like nowhere else."

With popular spots like Hoh Rainforest, Sol Duc Falls, and Lake Crescent, there are a lot of memories to be made here. World traveler and national park lover Tavia Carlson has this park at the top of her list of favorites because of its biodiversity. She says, "This park deserves all the time you can give it. If you want unforgettable waterfalls, diverse wildlife, and rugged natural beaches, this park is for you. A bonus: If you are a *Twilight* fan, you can add a day to explore all the *Twilight* spots in nearby Forks!"

Mick Dees agrees. To him, the lush rainforest vibes are hypnotic, and he can't get enough of the moss-covered old forests. "I love to get away from people and

Hoh Rain Forest is one of the main attractions at the park.

TRAILBLAZING!

There are almost 200 glaciers inside Olympic! The **Blue Glacier** is the largest in the park, and one of the most studied glaciers in the world. It's 2.6 miles long and descends from Mount Olympus, the highest peak in the Olympic Mountains.

Olympic National Park
Washington

find the quiet," he explains. "That silence, that natural peace in those forests, is a particular feeling I have rarely felt anywhere else in the world."

After a four-hour flight from Texas to Washington, Valerie and Eric Castillo, with their then 10-month-old daughter Journey in tow, hopped into their rental car for the drive to Olympic. As they reached the park, "We pulled up to Hoh Rainforest and it was raining outside. In our Hispanic culture, it's frowned upon to take your kids out in the rain or cold. So we waited in the car for a few hours hoping the rain would stop . . . and it didn't. I mean, it's a *rain*forest. It's not going to stop! We decided, let's just go. Let's get out of the car and let her get dirty. We had a suitcase full of clothing that we could put on her later, so we let her out in the rain and she jumped in. At the time, she was just learning how to walk so she was out there waddling in these puddles, slapping her hands in the water. It was such a great experience because we felt so much stronger at that point. We did not let the weather stop us from experiencing the park. I love that it builds our characters and the stories you tell people. Don't let the weather be the reason why you don't do things."

Keeping the rainy theme going, avid road-tripper and big-time national park enthusiast Bobby Beaulieu and his family have had a similarly moving experience. Olympic is their favorite park, and on their first trip, they spent their first night camping in the rainforest. As nighttime approached, a herd of elk passed through the campground, only a few feet away

Crowned the most picturesque waterfall in the park, the hike is less than a mile to reach Sol Duc Falls on a relatively level trail.

from them. "It was our first long road trip with our boys, and the first one sleeping in a tent. We didn't have a camp stove that year, so our cooking was done over the open campfire," Bobby says. In the morning, [my wife] cooked us blueberry pancakes in the rain over the fire." Other memorable animal sightings include their first banana slug, a mama deer with her fawn, marmots, and mountain goats.

Pacific Northwest & Alaska

Mount Rainier National Park

A glacier-capped volcano, subalpine meadows, and five major river systems help shape Mount Rainier National Park. The view of the massive stratovolcano is iconic and can be seen from miles away on a clear day. In spring, summer, fall, and winter, adventure awaits at this prominent peak in the Cascade Range.

Tavia Carlson is passionate about the national parks and has made it her life goal to experience all 63 "big" parks with her kids. A veteran whose husband is still actively serving in the military, Tavia often travels as a solo mom with her kids in tow. After years of visiting America's and Europe's big cities, she bought a campervan and took her two young kids on a six-week trip to a number of national parks. "We camped inside the parks, hiked small trails, found solitude and adventure within the park boundaries, and quickly developed a love for the National Park Service and exploring some of the most beautiful landscapes in the nation," she says.

One of her favorite memories was made at Mount Rainier. She visited the mountain with her family in June and they were surprised by the massive snow piles still covering the ground. Their plan to hike the Skyline Trail was up in the air since the trail was buried in two to three feet of snow, but Tavia says, "After some debate, we decided to go for it anyway. We were told it wasn't the right conditions for snowshoes or crampons, so we hiked in regular shoes. We made it about three miles before the trail completely disappeared into snow, so we turned around. What a day it was. We hiked through the snow with Mount Rainier as our backdrop and were greeted by huge white mountain goats, marmots, and bright sunny skies. On the way down, we were able to sit on our bums and slide down the mountain on some previously made snow slides. We also hiked the Grove of Patriarchs and a portion of the Silver Falls trail. The trip was magical and a core memory for us all."

Christa Eileen, a fellow national park lover who also strives to see all 63 national parks, visited Mount Rainier

ESTABLISHED	LOCATION
1899	Western Washington
SIZE	**VISITATION NO.**
369 square miles	1,674,294
LAND ACKNOWLEDGMENT	
Ancestral land of the Cowlitz, Muckleshoot, Nisqually, Puyallup, Squaxin Island, Yakama, and Coast Salish people	
FOR MORE INFO, VISIT:	
www.nps.gov/mora	

as her very first national park. She'd wanted to see the Pacific Northwest for a long time and it finally happened in the summer of 2016. "It's funny because at the time, I had no idea what the national park system was, to be honest, and I had only been on three hikes!" she shares. "I remember seeing Narada Falls, and at that point in my life, it was the largest waterfall I had ever seen in person. The size, the sound, and the spray of water were completely incredible to me and swallowed me whole with a desire to see every waterfall possible."

Christa admits that she's guilty of always wanting to hop on a plane to get a passport stamp, but the desire to visit all the national parks has really made her appreciate what we have in America. "The trips have not just been about seeing the parks, but have introduced me to so many different people, customs, and things I would have never been able to experience," she says.

During my early days of frequenting the national parks, I had a bodacious goal to climb Mount Rainier. After researching what it would take to

View of the Myrtle Falls braided cascade with the towering Mount Rainier in the background.

summit the volcano, I removed it from my bucket list. Mountaineering, putting on crampons, hiking with an ice axe, learning glacier-travel skills like how to self-arrest—I was more than happy to keep my feet on the ground.

But for Channel Islands' Superintendent Ethan McKinley, it was one of the best things he had done on the job. He once went up with the now Superintendent of Lake Mead National Recreation Area, at the time a Mount Rainier climbing ranger. "We had experienced a number of unusual storm events and had to go out to check on the mountain, make sure we could knock off any ice and check on things," he explains. "For us, going to climb mountains was like kids going to a candy shop. We were the only two people on Mount Rainier that day. So we got up to Camp Muir and just sat there in silence for about half an hour, taking in this expansive view and heard nothing but the wind. In those places, you can feel the whole gravity of the place. Then we skied back down. That's my first assignment out to a park, and if I had to look back and guess what the hook was, the thing that really made me say, okay, I'm going to sign up and be part of this, committing myself to this mission, I think that probably would have been it."

> **TRAILBLAZING!**
>
> **Mount Rainier** is the tallest volcano in the contiguous United States. It's a relatively young volcano, approximately 500,000 years old, and its last eruption is estimated to have occurred about 1,000 years ago.

Mount Rainier National Park
Washington

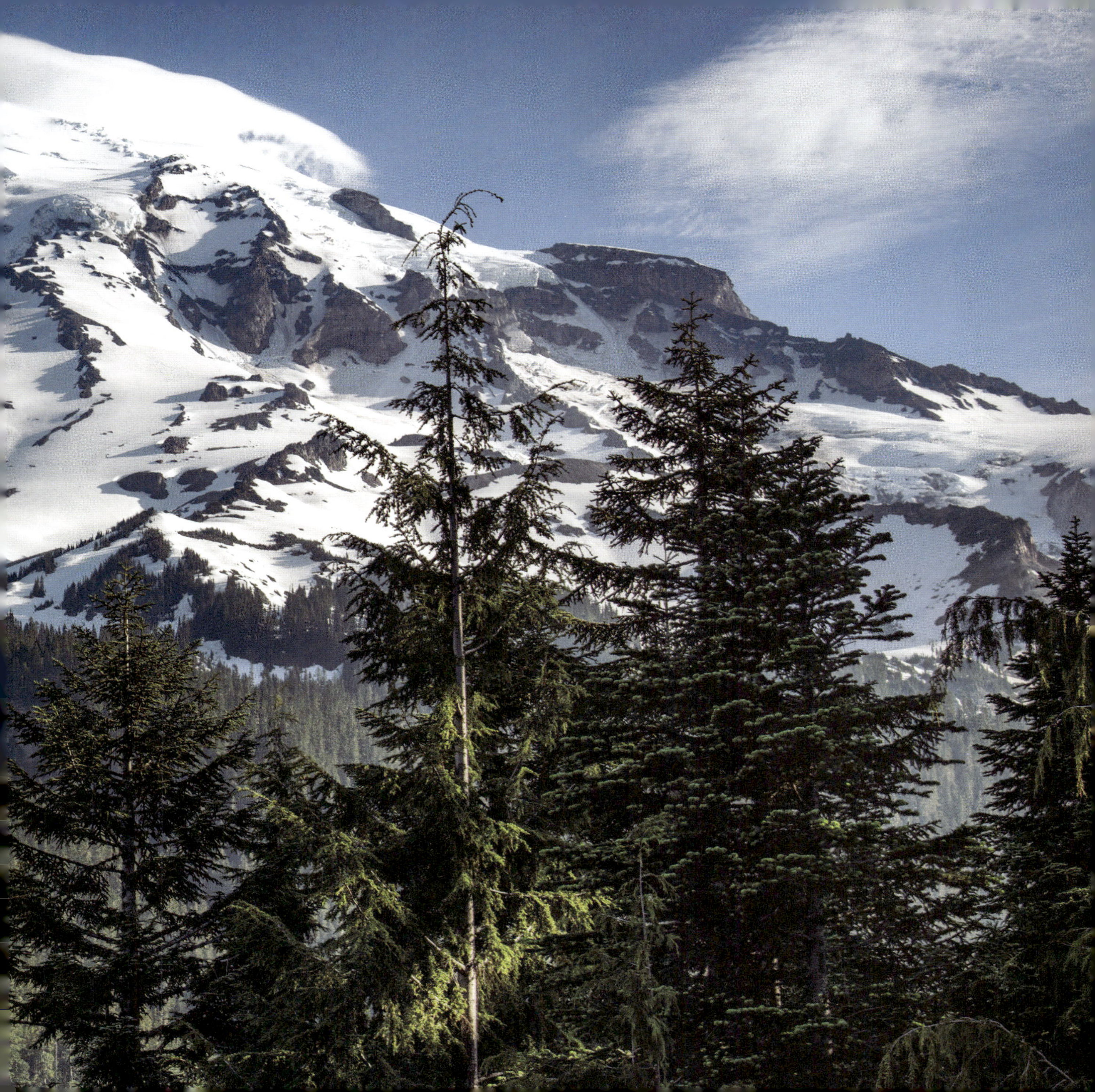

Pacific Northwest & Alaska

Crater Lake National Park

ESTABLISHED	LOCATION
1902	Southern Oregon
SIZE	VISITATION NO.
286 square miles	559,976

LAND ACKNOWLEDGMENT
Ancestral land of the Klamath (Makalak) people

FOR MORE INFO, VISIT:
www.nps.gov/crla

Part lake, part volcano, Crater Lake National Park has some of the bluest water you'll ever see. Formed atop the collapsed Mount Mazama volcano, the remarkable color and clarity of the water is a result of a lack of suspended particles in the water. There is also another volcano inside the caldera, known as Wizard Island.

Phantom Ship Island is a remnant of an ancient volcanic cone, displaying the oldest rock in the Crater Lake basin (over 400,000 years old!).

The first thing that came to Brandi Small's mind when she saw the sign at Crater Lake National Park's entrance was how excited she was, despite not fully knowing what to expect (besides the blue lake). "The drive was so nice and calming. Just being there was amazing," she says. But the best memory "was the family members I went with. They wanted to make sure we enjoyed it and appreciated this park that was near us."

Though maybe not memorable in a good way, what Brandi remembers from her hike down the Cleetwood Cove Trail to get to the lake was being eaten up by the mosquitoes. Still, that didn't take away from how beautiful the scenery was or the wonderful company she had on that trip. Brandi, an outdoor enthusiast, just simply loves being outside: "It really helps with my anxiety. I feel so free when I get to play outside. Camping is just hands down the best way to wake up outside and watch the forest or desert come alive. For me, hiking is so calming and I can do it every day. It's something you

Red Indian Paintbrush painting the landscape of Crater Lake National Park in the summer.

can enjoy alone or with people. It calms all my worries; it is my happy place."

Some of her favorite spots at Crater Lake are the trail that leads you down to the lake, views from the Sinnott Memorial Overlook by the caldera rim, and the famous Phantom Ship Overlook, providing one of the best views of Phantom Ship Island.

One great thing to know for pet parents is that pets are welcome at this park, unlike at many other national parks. Leashed pets are allowed at the Mazama and Lost Creek Campgrounds, all picnic areas, on established roads, within 50 feet of paved surfaces, and on several designated trails (check the park's website for the latest information). Crater Lake is also a favorite for Genevieve Lei, a national park lover who is halfway through her bucket list to visit all the 63 parks, because pets are allowed, so she was able to visit the park with her pup Ranger during a road trip to his first national park.

Crater Lake National Park sits at an elevation above 6,000 feet, so the weather can change rather quickly. Fellow national park lover Chris Zayas experienced this firsthand during her visit to the park, which started out hot and sunny. "As we started up the road it became more overcast and soon began to snow," she relates. "By the time we reached the viewing area for Crater Lake, it was in the low forties and snowing! We scrambled

In the national parks, even outhouses offer a gorgeous view!

to unpack the back of the van enough to reach our suitcases and find some warm clothing. We changed clothes in the visitor center. Although Crater Lake didn't show off its beautiful indigo blue water that day, it was still an adventure and the park itself was lovely."

My recollections of Crater Lake are a mixed bag. I had initially planned for a three-day summer weekend at the Mazama Campground with a couple of my park-loving friends. One thing about visiting this park in the summer is that you need to be wary of forest fires, and one did break out a few weeks before my trip. Then, a few days before my trip, I received news of the passing of my "American dad." The funeral would be in Oklahoma on the last day of my trip. I decided to cut the trip a day short so I could enjoy Crater Lake and still attend the funeral.

After setting up camp, my friends and I caught the Wizard Island boat tour. The tour was narrated by a park ranger, and it remains the best way to learn about the park in a short amount of time. The boat also stopped at Wizard Island, allowing visitors to hop off to go for a swim or hike the Wizard Island Summit Trail. (Rangers often recommend securing your boat tickets prior to your visit, as they can sell out fast during the summer and there are only a limited number of tickets for sale 24 hours prior to tour time.) On that trip, we also checked out the pinnacles spires at the end of Pinnacles Road, an interesting geologic feature for those who love rocks, geology, and anything volcanoes. For a future return visit, I have the Crater Lake Trolley tour on my to-do list, so I can focus on the views without worrying about being behind the wheel!

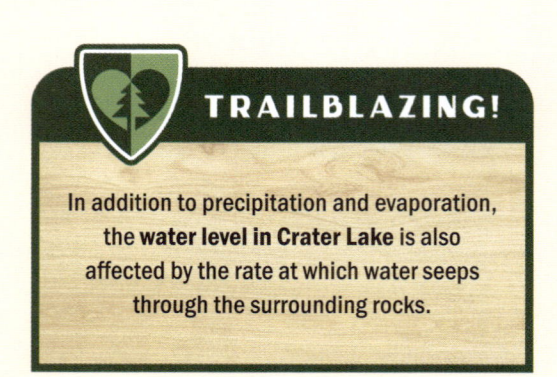

TRAILBLAZING!

In addition to precipitation and evaporation, the **water level in Crater Lake** is also affected by the rate at which water seeps through the surrounding rocks.

Crater Lake National Park
Oregon

Great Basin National Park
Nevada

Western

Mountains, oceans, and deserts can all be found in the iconic Western region. California, the largest state in this region, is home to the highest mountain peak in the contiguous United States, the lowest point in North America, and both the largest and tallest known trees in the world. In parks across the Pacific Ocean, you'll find a series of shield volcanoes, one of which is the largest active volcano on Earth and another the biggest mountain in the world when measured from the base below sea level all the way to the top. If that doesn't impress you, perhaps a grand view of one of the seven natural wonders of the world found in Arizona might.

Western

Redwood National Park

ESTABLISHED	LOCATION
1968	Northern California coast

SIZE	VISITATION NO.
206 square miles	409,105

LAND ACKNOWLEDGMENT
Ancestral land of the Yurok, Hupa, Tolowa, and Karuk people

FOR MORE INFO, VISIT:
www.nps.gov/redw

Featuring more than just coastal redwood forests, Redwood National and State Park is also home to vast prairies, oak woodlands, and miles of rugged coastline. Consisting of Redwood National Park and three California state parks (Del Norte Coast Redwoods State Park, Jedediah Smith Redwoods State Park, and Prairie Creek Redwoods State Park), this complex is co-managed by the National Park Service and the California Department of Parks and Recreation along with tribal leaders from the Indigenous communities surrounding the area.

Redwood National Park is home to the tallest tree in the world, but it also feels like home to Ranger Serena Sinclair. Despite growing up in Southern California, she had only been to Grand Canyon National Park prior to joining the National Park Service as a Volunteer In Park (VIP) during her adult years. A female park ranger from her Grand Canyon visit made a lasting impression on young Serena, who left wondering if she too could grow up to become a ranger. It was a dream she left unpursued for many years.

"When I was 44, my little brother passed away and I had been suffering from severe depression for many years," Serena recounts. "I went camping for five months in Monterey and Santa Cruz, and I noticed that being outdoors had lifted my fog of depression and I really didn't know why at the time. While I was camping, I met a park ranger that I deeply respected and admired, and I thought again to myself, could I become a park ranger now? But I quickly dismissed the thought because my life has taken a different path. And then I started asking about free camping in the State Park system, and I became a park aide to get free camping. And it was at that time, working at Henry Cowell Redwoods State Park

Fog accounts for roughly 40 percent of redwood's moisture intake.

in the Santa Cruz Mountains, I found out that 96 percent of the old-growth trees have been harvested and only 4 percent remained. I had to tell the world about redwoods. I wanted everybody to fall in love with the redwoods like I had."

Ranger Serena loves meeting people as she roves the park, answering inquisitive questions and making meaningful connections with visitors. Her passion lies in the healing properties of the forest, as she has personally experienced those powerful forces. At Redwood, she hosts a ranger program introducing park lovers to biophilia, which suggests humans possess an innate tendency to connect with nature and other forms of life. "It's the love of life and deep connections with nature, it has many health benefits," she says. "I talk a little bit about integrating nature into personal spaces, your home and your office, before going over ecotherapy learning and its role in promoting mental health through nature-based interventions. And then we go on a guided nature walk where we just immerse ourselves and all our senses, tasting some of the plants and berries, listening, and touching. Not just using our sight, but all our senses."

One of her favorite trails is the Simpson-Reed Trail located in Jedediah Smith State Park, via which you enter an ancient redwood forest aged a thousand years old that forms a towering canopy overshadowing a wide variety of ground cover, such as ferns, hemlocks, and nurse logs. Another is the Berry Glen Trail in Redwood National Park, which is a bit less traveled. We're both

Prepare to get your feet wet and walk the Fern Canyon Trail (permit required).

Redwood National Park
California

Though perhaps best known for trees, Redwood also boasts 40 miles of rugged coastline.

fans of the Lady Bird Johnson Grove Trail in Redwood and Stout Grove Trail at Jedediah Smith. For a drive-through forest bathing experience, don't miss Newton B. Drury Scenic Parkway, a ten-mile alternative to U.S. 101, and Howland Hill Road, a mostly unpaved 10-mile road (not suitable for RVs and trailers) for an intimate encounter with the towering old-growth redwoods.

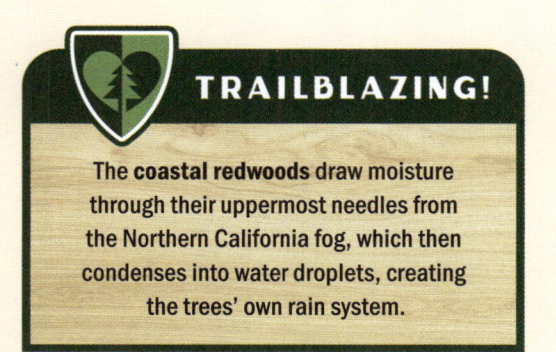

TRAILBLAZING!

The **coastal redwoods** draw moisture through their uppermost needles from the Northern California fog, which then condenses into water droplets, creating the trees' own rain system.

The best things about Redwood National and State Park for Ranger Serena are its healing power and the resiliency of the redwoods. "I had to be resilient, just like these trees," she shares. "I see the damage that they've been through, the trauma that they've been through. They have a stable root system and they're still supporting their family members. I feel like I had to do the same thing and show my family how to grieve in a healthy way."

Redwood National and State Parks was the first national park Amanda Bauler visited, when she was 15. "I grew up in the Midwest and was amazed by the size of the trees and the moodiness of the misty forest as I hiked through them with friends," she remembers. "We tent-camped on the beach near the park (but someone in the group rented a hotel room and all the teenage girls headed there to get a warm shower and to wash our hair). We spent the next morning tide-pooling along the rocky coastline seeing so many creatures I'd only seen before in an aquarium."

Amanda's family's love affair with national parks started in 2010, when they went on a trip southwest to visit a number of national parks. "We discovered the Junior Ranger program and my daughters loved them, so we decided to explore as many parks as we could on that trip (both big and small). They came home with twelve badges and a fantastic new hobby. When I saw how much they loved exploring the history and beautiful outdoor spaces preserved in our parks, I wanted to make sure we made more memories together in the parks."

Western

Lassen Volcanic National Park

The popular hike to Bumpass Hell descends 200 feet into the basin, providing access to the parks' largest hydrothermal area.

Home to the largest plug dome volcano in the world, Lassen Volcanic National Park has many hydrothermal features, without the Yellowstone crowds. One of the most unique features of the park is that all four primary types of volcanoes can be found within the park boundaries. Though it's still a geological hotspot, the park is more than just fumaroles and volcanic rocks. Mountain meadows, alpine lakes, and waterfalls await visitors in summer and fall.

Growing up, Ranger Jim Richardson was a Boy Scout who camped regularly, and his family went on annual vacations to national parks across the country. He and his family enjoy natural and historical areas. His first national park as a seasonal (and later permanent) ranger was Rocky Mountain National Park, where he thrived on the chance to climb, ski, horse pack, and

A sunset view at Manzanita Lake, with Lassen Peak towering in the background.

ESTABLISHED	LOCATION
1916	Northern California
SIZE	**VISITATION NO.**
166 square miles	418,978

LAND ACKNOWLEDGMENT
Ancestral land of the Atsugewi, Yana, Yahi and Mountain Maidu people

FOR MORE INFO, VISIT:
www.nps.gov/lavo

perform technical rescue. Years later, his journey with the National Park Service has now taken him to another mountain park, albeit volcanic, and as a superintendent this time.

After years of being at Lassen Volcanic National Park, Superintendent Jim has a good understanding of what visitors love and look for at the park. As such, he makes sure to assign adequate resources to complete projects that prioritize visitor safety and enjoyment. When asked about his favorite part of the park, Superintendent Jim shares with excitement "the true wilderness aspect of so much of the park. I, or any member of the public, can park alongside the busy park highway and just wander away. In ten minutes, you feel like you are in the real wilderness!"

The park offers a variety of activities that vary by season and certain roads or sections are open at different times of the year. All the park's roads are usually open in summer and fall, but since the park is situated at a higher elevation, the main road cutting through it is closed during winter and spring. Looking on the bright (and snowy) side, winter brings opportunities to snowshoe, sled, snowplay, cross-country ski, and backcountry ski or snowboard.

Superintendent Jim loves wandering into the wilderness. "For a destination hike, my go-to is to Bumpass Hell," he says. "This is a three-mile hike on a well-maintained trail to the most diverse hydrothermal area in the park with great interpretive signs and a boardwalk to get you close to the action." As for me, I love the hikes onto the four types of volcanoes. You can hike on a shield volcano via Prospect Peak, a plug dome volcano via Lassen Peak, a composite volcano via Brokeoff Mountain, and a cinder cone volcano via Cinder Cone by Butte Lake area. Put it on your bucket list!

> **TRAILBLAZING!**
>
> **Bumpass Hell** is named after Kendall V. Bumpass, who wandered around the hydrothermal area—and into thin-crust ground, burning his foot. He returned later with a reporter for a tour, only to break through the ground again at another spot and plunge into a boiling spring. He survived, but his leg did not.

Boiling Springs Lake has a number of steam vents located underwater that keeps the lake's temperature around 125°F.

Western

Yosemite National Park

ESTABLISHED	LOCATION
1890	Sierra Nevada, Northern California
SIZE	VISITATION NO.
1,160 square miles	3,897,070
LAND ACKNOWLEDGMENT	
Ancestral land of the Ahwahneechee people from the Southern Sierra Miwok	
FOR MORE INFO, VISIT:	
www.nps.gov/yose	

Loved by many, Yosemite National Park is as iconic as national parks get, featuring granite cathedrals, spectacular waterfalls, and more than 800 miles of hiking trails with unsurpassed views of the Sierra Nevada beauty.

Scott Gediman has wanted to be a park ranger at Yosemite since his family vacations at the park every year. He went to San Diego State University to pursue his degree in journalism and public relations before finding his way into the National Park Service.

Ranger Scott started his career as a park ranger in Glen Canyon National Recreation Area before getting hired as permanent ranger at Grand Canyon National Park. Several years later, he jumped at the first opportunity to work at Yosemite, and has now been at the park for almost thirty years. A lot has changed since then, but the beauty of Yosemite prevails. "It's a beautiful national park," he says. "So many of the superlatives: one of the tallest waterfalls in North America, El Capitan, the largest granite monoliths. I think Yosemite in so many ways just epitomizes the national park system. It's where the idea for national parks came from, and so much of everything from the architecture to the history to the association with the Indigenous tribes in and

View of Half Dome from Glacier Point.

Yosemite National Park
Nevada and California

around the park. There's just so much of Yosemite that embodies the national park idea that I love so much and feel so privileged to represent each day."

Some of his favorite trails are the ones that offer classic Yosemite experiences, like the Mist Trail, which offers views of Vernal Falls and Nevada Falls. The trail gets busy in summer, so if you plan to experience this one, try going on a weekday for a more manageable crowd. Yosemite gets busy starting in June, coinciding with the summer school break. Pro tip from Ranger Scott on how to have a good visit at this busy national park is to consider coming during the off-season in spring, fall, or winter. If the driving or parking situation frustrates you, I recommend taking Amtrak's San Joaquin line to Merced station and transferring to Amtrak Thruway Bus Route 15, which takes you directly into Yosemite Valley. While in the park, you can move around the valley area via the free park shuttle, which stops near the popular spots.

Tavia Carlson loves Yosemite for many reasons, primarily its accessibility. "You can see some of America's most iconic views without hiking," she notes. "This means everyone is able to experience Tunnel View and Glacier Point. Yosemite also has many activities, like renting bikes and ice skating in the valley. You can tent camp, glamp, or stay at the historic Ahwahnee Hotel. The park caters to everyone with any budget or ability."

Corey Ford, another national park lover and a fellow 63-park bucket lister who loves Yosemite more than anyone I know, cherishes the special moments made at

Horsetail Fall illuminated by the sunset.

the park, like capturing the unique Horsetail Fall Firefall. In February, when conditions are right, this natural phenomenon sets the waterfall "ablaze" about five to fifteen minutes before sunset.

A big bucket-list hike at this park is the famous Half Dome hike. Winning the permit lottery is half the

TRAILBLAZING!

The Buffalo Soldiers, an all-black regiment established by Congress after the Civil War, served as some of the earliest protectors of Yosemite, which helped create the modern model for park management.

battle, and hiking your way up (and down) the granite monolith is the other half. Damian Vujicic and his son Austin won the lottery and flew to California all the way from Australia to check it off their bucket list. "We flew 14 hours from Melbourne to Los Angeles and then immediately drove to El Portal, only to wake up the following morning at two o'clock to begin our trek. Months of hard work and determination at the local fitness center worked in our favor as we made our way up. Upon reaching the cables, storm clouds rolled in . . . And we were sadly not able to continue. Devastated is an understatement. We looked around at others in the same boat as us and reminded ourselves of where we were, in Yosemite National Park, and what it took to be there. We were grateful for America the beautiful."

Mary Quan, a national park lover and a dear friend of mine, started her national park adventures in Yosemite two years after getting divorced, following 25 years of marriage. "I just couldn't believe the beauty of the park," she shares. "For the first time in my adult life, experiencing being able to camp in a national park that was so beautiful, in a tent, I remember being blown away by the sights of nature. I would become excited like a little kid if we saw any sort of wildlife. That's what got me started on this journey. I remember taking a walk down one of the trails like it was yesterday, looking at these beautiful massive trees and it really brought me to tears. I had never experienced anything so beautiful."

The hype is real when it comes to Yosemite, the kind that you have to be there to experience it yourself. Ranger Scott says, "We love the visitors. I feel that there's no substitute to experiencing Yosemite. You can watch a video, you can read a book, you can watch anything about the parks, but being in the parks and experiencing them in person, there's no substitute for it. I love to welcome the park visitors. Yosemite has been called the crown jewels of the National Park system, I think there's a good reason for that."

Another view of Half Dome.

Yosemite National Park
Nevada and California

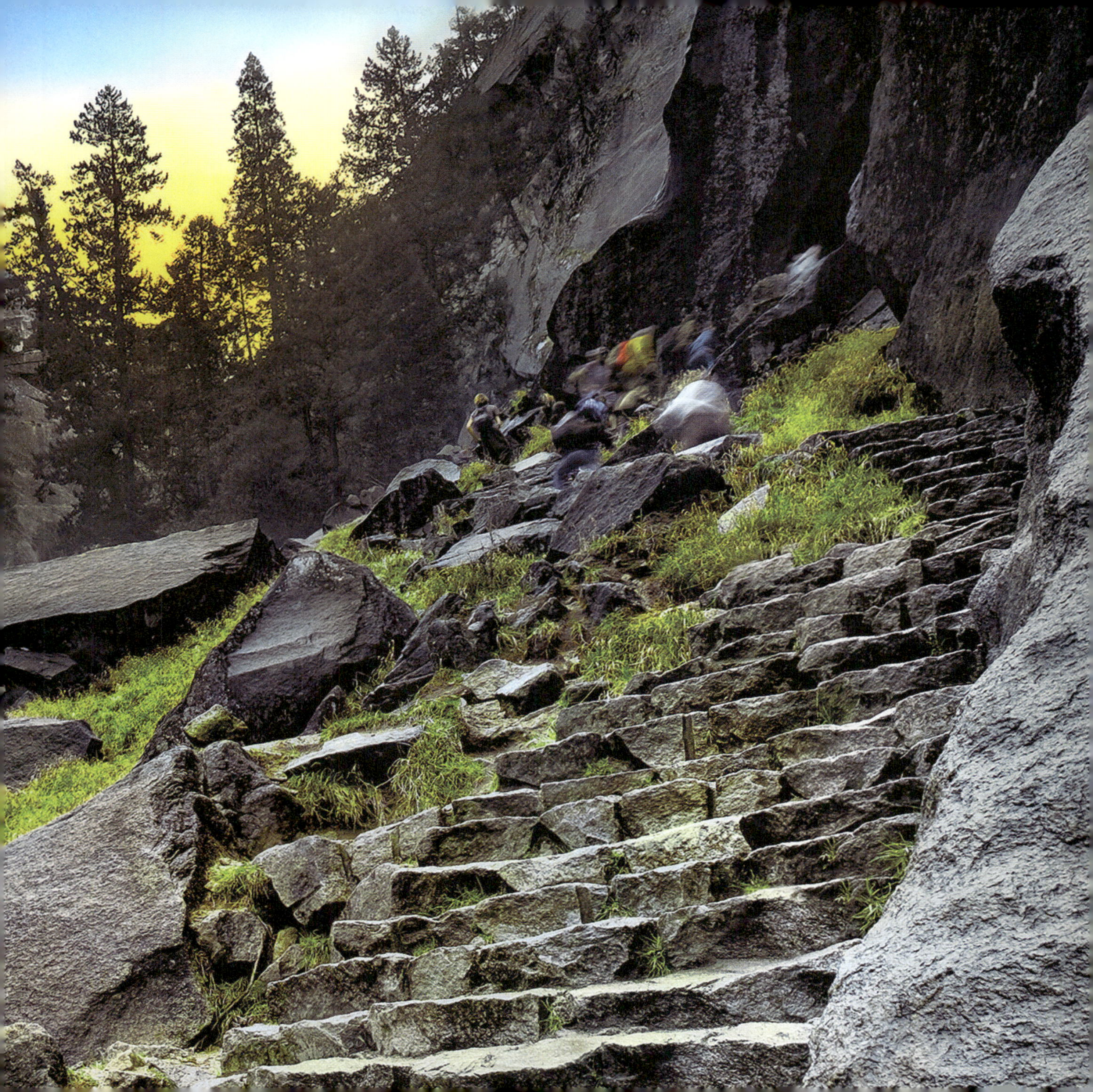

Western

Kings Canyon National Park

ESTABLISHED	LOCATION
1940	Central-East California

SIZE	VISITATION NO.
772 square miles	643,065

LAND ACKNOWLEDGMENT

Ancestral land of the Mono and Yokut people

FOR MORE INFO, VISIT:

www.nps.gov/seki

A visit to Kings Canyon National Park is often paired with a trip to Sequoia National Park to see the big trees. Both the General Grant tree in Kings Canyon and the General Sherman tree in Sequoia are impressive to witness in person. But what sets Kings Canyon National Park apart from its neighbor is its namesake, a rugged, glacier-carved valley more than a mile deep.

Kings River flows through the park, traversing one of the deepest canyons in North America.

Enza Vujicic began visiting national parks as a ten-year-old Australian transplant living in Seattle, Washington. Her very first national park was the majestic Mount Rainier back in 1986. After moving back to Australia and making many return visits to the United States, she finally found her way back to America's Best Idea in 2011. This time, she visited Death Valley National Park with her husband, Damian, and their children, Austin and Veronica. "[Damian and I were] in awe of the desert's dry, vast landscape. A visit to Zabriske point on a 124°F day in August 2011 was an eye-opener. Beauty could be dangerous too."

In December 2015, the family returned to America for more national park visits. They drove all day from Las Vegas to get to Kings Canyon. "It was dark, snowing, and the road guide was the reflection of deer eyes around every twist and turn," she recalls. "We pulled up safely to the Grant Grove cabins where we were greeted with walls of snow and the dim light of the check-in. After a warm night's sleep, we woke up to glistening fresh snow and

Snow-covered sequoia trees during the quiet winter season.

Kings Canyon National Park was one of my favorites when I first visited all the National Park Service sites in California. What draws me to this park isn't the big trees, but the canyon itself. A trip to Kings Canyon without going down into the canyon section feels incomplete, as you miss visiting one of the most beautiful meadows found in national parks: the Zumwalt Meadow. I still remember the moment I first laid eyes on the meadow and stared at North Dome. The beauty, peace, and solace I found there brought tears to my eyes. Another core memory at this park is thru-hiking the John Muir Trail. As I hiked down Glen Pass, I stopped several times, not just to give my knees and ankles a break from stepping down the trail's large "stair steps," but also to take in the beauty of the landscape. Never have I ever seen such a magnificent display of exposed metamorphic rocks.

But don't just take my word for it. Have your own backcountry experience in this amazing scenery via Rae Lakes Loop!

silence. Our family promptly dressed and hiked down to the awe-inspiring General Grant tree. We had this monolith to ourselves."

The experience left Enza and Damian longing to see more of the US and national parks around the world, and they set out to do just that. "We spread the word that the United States is more, much more, than Hollywood and politics," she says. "The national parks annual pass system is an inexpensive way to see the most beautiful natural wonders of the world."

TRAILBLAZING!

Kings Canyon is said to be the deepest canyon in the US. Measured from Spanish Peak down to the confluence of the Middle and South Forks of the Kings River, it is 8,200 feet deep.

Western
Sequoia National Park

If you're ever struggling with something and feel that you just need to take a step back and reassess, spending time gazing at the gentle giants in Sequoia National Park will help you put things into perspective. Sequoia is home to the largest tree (by volume) on Earth, General Sherman, which stands proudly at 275 feet tall and 36 feet in diameter at the base. This park will make you feel small, and may shift your perspective about your worries and woes.

Sequoia was Karen Aranda's first national park. She visited with her family when she was living in California. "I remember driving up the roads through the sequoias and we pulled off to the side of the road to take in the views and smell of the forest," she recalls. "At the time, my family wasn't aware that this was a national park. They were just aiming to go somewhere outside and enjoy the fresh air. I guess that's where my siblings and I got the traveling and exploring bug, especially my sister and me."

For Mick Dees, it's not all about the big trees. Finding mule deer on park grounds is his favorite Sequoia memory. "As a wildlife photographer, I was taken in by the little mule deer that lived beneath the trees. I found a little family of them, mom, dad, and two fawns feeding on the plants, playing in the shrubbery, and climbing on fallen giant sequoias," he says. "My time that day was 90 percent focused on that family of deer rather than the impressive sequoias, and I don't regret it one bit."

I've dubbed Sequoia National Park as my "home park," because it's the closest national park to where I live here in California. It's one of the two parks that I often take visiting friends and family to, since it's a two-hour drive away and I know they won't find views like what Sequoia has to offer anywhere else. On one of my first visits, I took my friends Kelsi Goss and Tamar Saunders for a day trip on a sunny winter afternoon. Kelsi had been to Grand Canyon National Park once, making Sequoia her second national park, and she was

ESTABLISHED	LOCATION
1890	Central-East California
SIZE	VISITATION NO.
631 square miles	980,567
LAND ACKNOWLEDGMENT	
Ancestral land of the Foothill Yokut, Tübatulabal, Paiute, and Western Mono (Monache) people	
FOR MORE INFO, VISIT:	
For more info: www.nps.gov/seki	

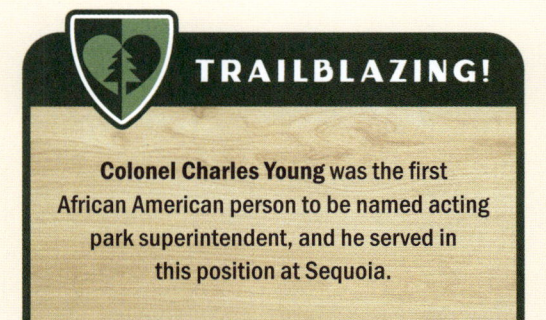

> ### TRAILBLAZING!
> **Colonel Charles Young** was the first African American person to be named acting park superintendent, and he served in this position at Sequoia.

in awe of the giant trees. That trip inspired a return visit a few years later, with her family of four.

For Kelsi, the scale of the sequoia trees—an unfamiliar sight on the East Coast where she grew up—really blew her mind. "I had no idea they could actually be that big," she says. "My first visit was also really special [because] I got to share it with Linda and Tamar. Something about exploring trails with close friends just makes the experience even more fun. The three of us joke around a lot, so many of my photos are pretty goofy. It's fun to look back and revisit the awe I had of that place, as well as all of the laughs the three of us had together. When I returned to the park with my family, it was really fun to see the boys enjoy nature and even start requesting that I take certain photos of them. It's always fun to see how the parks can be an opportunity to enjoy nature, get some exercise in, but also learn so much about what the landscape of our country has to offer."

Sequoia National Park was also where Tigran Nahabedian, a young public land advocate who spent his childhood years volunteering at national parks, found the most peaceful campsite and had his first bear sightings. Trees, meadows, waterfalls, wildlife, and even a marble cavern (check out Crystal Cave), this park has them all.

The iconic trees in Sequoia National Park.

Sequoia National Park
California

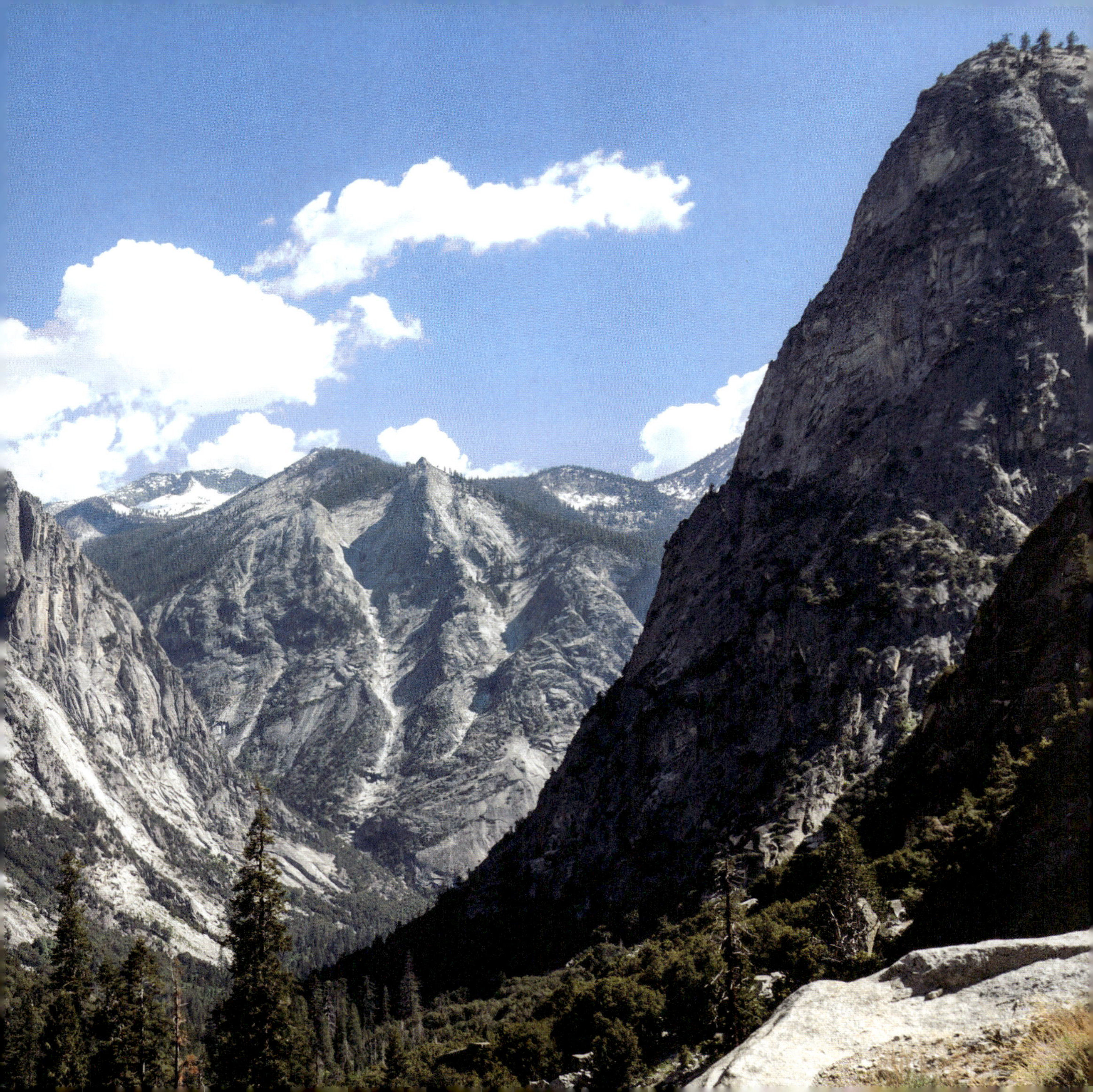

Western

Pinnacles National Park

Spectacular sunset over the towering pinnacles.

Small but mighty, Pinnacles National Park is known for its California condor recovery program, but the park has even more to offer. With talus caves, bat habitats, and volcanic rocks (my two favorites combined), the park is aptly named for its towering pinnacles that rise out of the ground.

Ranger Rich Moore is amazed by how lush and green the scenery gets in the Gabilan Range. "What makes Pinnacles special is its proximity to people while also having incredible resources. You might be able to find more hiking trails, darker night skies, diverse flora and fauna at other parks, but many of those sites may not be as close to the population that Pinnacles has access to. When we think about nurturing the next generation of stewards, a big part of that is experiencing the parks firsthand, and many people can do that at Pinnacles."

Though Pinnacles is relatively the least-visited national park in California, that doesn't necessarily mean the park is not busy. Ranger Rich recommends arriving early, especially when visiting on weekends. Bring enough food and water to last your trip, since your only option to refuel in the park is the campground store on the east side. Like many national parks, cell phone service may be limited in some areas, so plan your activities in advance and download the official National Park Service app to better navigate the park. "Bring a headlamp!" he advises. "There are two caves in the park that are very popular, and the flashlight on your phone does not really work that well."

Pinnacles National Park inspired Patrick Rodden a national park lover who photographs his way through the parks, to begin volunteering for the National Park

ESTABLISHED	LOCATION
1908 (redesignated 2013)	Central California
SIZE	**VISITATION NO.**
42 square miles	341,220
LAND ACKNOWLEDGMENT	
Ancestral land of the Chalon and Mutsun people	
FOR MORE INFO, VISIT:	
www.nps.gov/pinn	

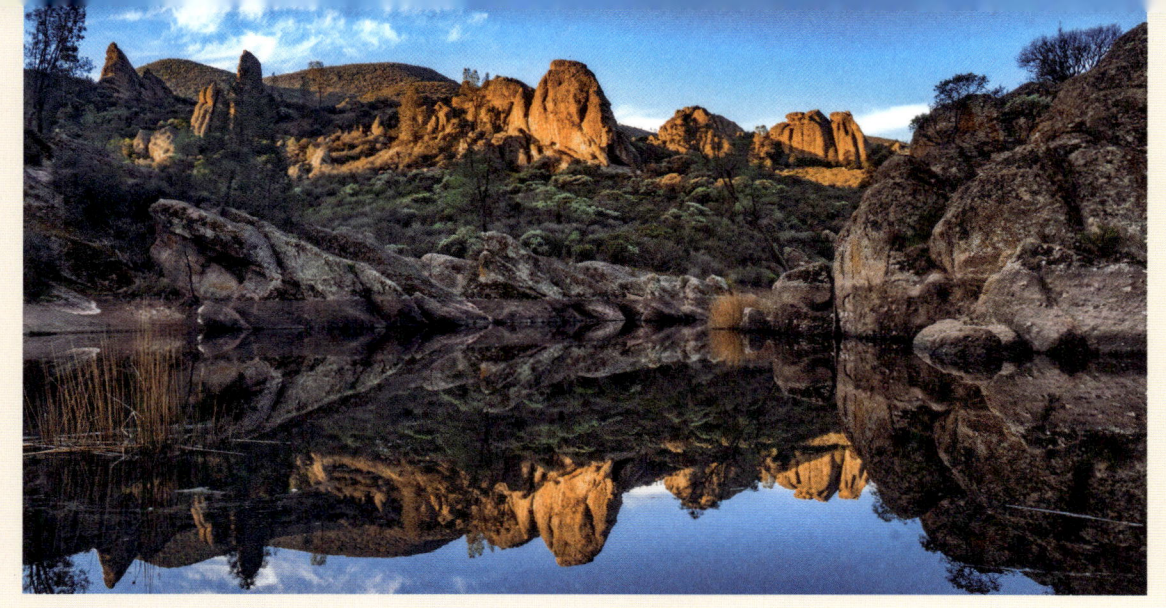

Beautiful reflection at the Bear Gulch Reservoir, a mile hike up the Moses Spring Trail.

Service. He was tasked with assisting visitors at the Bear Gulch Nature Center in the park. "My duties included teaching people about the California condor, checking wildflower status, teaching about park geology, and helping people with hikes and safe practices," he shares. "My favorite part of the park is visiting the west entrance. From that vantage point, you can see all the pinnacles in their glory. The intrigue of Pinnacles to me is the fact that the Neenach Formation moved all the way up the coast via the San Andreas Fault, and ended up where they are today. The power of the Earth is visible while hiking through the park."

Pinnacles is also special for a fellow national park lover, Genevieve Lei, for a very personal reason. "My now-husband proposed to me at Pinnacles on the High Peaks Trail," she shares. "On the way back down from the hike, it started raining lightly. If you're superstitious, I've read it's good luck and signifies a cleansing in tough times or sadness in the past."

This park is also where I first met Gen, her then-boyfriend Paul, and her best friend Brandy, along with my friend Mary, back in 2017. It was the start of many national park meetups for several years, before the pandemic put a pause on our adventure streaks.

TRAILBLAZING!

A **talus cave** is formed when rockfalls fill an existing steep, narrow canyon with boulders. The talus caves at Pinnacles are believed to have formed during the last ice age.

Western

Death Valley National Park

The name may have given it away, but Death Valley National Park is best described as a land of extremes. Extreme heat, extreme elevation, and extreme landscapes all add up to create the largest national park in the lower 48 of the United States. Death Valley is also the very first national park established to preserve the desert, a landscape that was often seen as an inhospitable and threatening wasteland.

Having been born to parents who spent years working for the National Park Service, national parks have been a familiar space for Ranger Matthew Lamar. He grew up visiting many of the national historic sites on the East Coast, and as a lover of history and national parks, becoming a park ranger was a natural career path.

Ranger Matthew found his way to Death Valley through his seasonal assignment out west. "My first couple of jobs with the Park Service, I was at parks like Rocky Mountain National Park, where I had a variety of experiences. It has everything you want in a classic national park; the mountains, the elk, and moose. I thought nothing was going to beat that. But then I got

ESTABLISHED	LOCATION
1933 (redesignated 1994)	Eastern California and Nevada
SIZE	**VISITATION NO.**
5,312 square miles	1,099,632
LAND ACKNOWLEDGMENT	
Ancestral land of the Timbisha Shoshone people	
FOR MORE INFO, VISIT:	
www.nps.gov/deva	

The Mesquite Flat Sand Dunes are known for dramatic shadows at both sunrise and sunset.

TRAILBLAZING!

Death Valley holds the record for being **the hottest place on Earth!** A temperature of 134°F was recorded there on July 10, 1913. Earlier that year, the park also recorded its lowest temperature, 15°F.

the job in Death Valley, and over the course of those six months, I really fell in love with the area and realized that, yes, it's so different from the Rocky Mountains, but for me it was just so special. There is so much to love about Death Valley but the potential for solitude, to experience the wilderness, to really feel like no one has hiked this mountain this year or maybe even this decade, that's a really special feeling. I really appreciate that aspect and the ability to get away, which is something that's really hard to do at some parks."

You may have heard that "half the park is after dark," and that couldn't be truer in Death Valley. As a certified international dark sky park, thanks to its remoteness, the park is a fantastic place to stargaze. The parks hosts a dark sky festival in February each year—and it is a serious business. "There are a lot of other parks that do star parties or night festivals, but ours is pretty unique because not only are we one of the largest international dark sky parks in the world, but because of our extreme environment, we also have been an analog for other worlds like Mars and all these new moons and planets within our solar system," Ranger Matthew says. "Scientists studied Death Valley to better understand the other world. NASA has come here and tested the Curiosity Rover and the Perseverance Rover. During the festival, we celebrate the dark night sky and all the important values the park plays in understanding other planets."

Death Valley weather is extreme, with a 120°F temperature quite regular during the summer months.

The Badwater Basin salt flats mark the lowest point in North America, 282 feet below sea level.

Death Valley National Park
California and Nevada

The colorful hills of Artists Palette in Death Valley.

While there are some people who want to experience that level of heat, it does limit what you can do at the parks, especially if you plan to hit the trails. One must-see recommendation from Ranger Matthew is for visitors to stop by the Badwater Basin, the lowest place in North America. "It's very cool to see the salt flats out there," he says. "Even more beautiful if you walk out to the polygon pattern and see them up close."

For Ranger Matthew, this is his favorite national park. "It's so large and so much of it is wilderness, so it's really easy to get away and find a space for yourself. I love hiking here and the fact that I can go exploring every weekend and I still probably won't be able to see everything that this park has to offer between the beautiful canyon, the human history, and the mining history. You never know what you're going to stumble across, so it keeps you engaged and interested. To be able to look up and see the Milky Way, it's something I don't take for granted."

As for me, Death Valley is the national park where I kicked off my initial California national park bucket list. It also could have been my last national park, had I not swiftly recovered from the heat exhaustion while hiking the strenuous eight-mile "Complete Circuit." The trail starts at Zabriskie Point, passes through the Gower Gulch, reaches Golden Canyon—and then you have to hike back. A rookie hiker and a national park novice back then, I arrived at the park at midday and started my first hike in the desert at noon, when the temperature was 100°F in the spring. Keep in mind when you're checking the temperatures for Death Valley online, the number you're reading can be 10°F to 20°F lower than the actual temperature on the valley floor.

I make a return visit to Death Valley every year during the first weekend of April, for what I call my "parkniversary" trip. I typically invite some park-loving friends to join me at my group campsite for a day full of desert hikes and a night filled with stars.

Western

Channel Islands National Park

Often called the Galapagos Islands of California, Channel Islands National Park consists of five of the eight Channel Islands located off the coast of Southern California. These islands have never been connected to the mainland, which makes them the perfect home to 140 species that are endemic to the Channel Islands. Kelp forests, sea caves, and pristine beaches await!

Ranger Ethan McKinley was first introduced to this park more than a decade ago by a park ranger friend who worked there. They kayaked, backpacked, and camped on Santa Cruz Island. Ethan fell in love. Little did he know, he would return several years later as the Channel Islands National Park Superintendent. "It's really a dream job to be responsible for these islands and a huge responsibility at the same time," he says. "At first, I assumed you had a group of islands off the coast of the Los Angeles area, it must be overrun. Must be built and developed. The audacity to think that we could go back from a previous generation of how we treated land and recover a place that just makes your heart soar. If you think about the human element of the management of the islands, that's where it's at for me. The basic

The iconic Arch Rock and the lighthouse, symbols of Anacapa and Channel Islands National Park.

ESTABLISHED	LOCATION
1980	Off the coast of Southern California
SIZE	**VISITATION NO.**
390 square miles	328,746
LAND ACKNOWLEDGMENT	
Ancestral land of the Chumash people	
FOR MORE INFO, VISIT:	
www.nps.gov/chis	

premise of it is such an exercise in hope and it's been taken so seriously that it became a reality."

Getting to the Channel Islands isn't as hard as deciding which island to visit and planning your visit around the boat schedules. Superintendent Ethan sees it as an inner island/outer island experience. "Anacapa or Santa Cruz Islands are lovely places to spend some time getting to know the geology and the ecosystems that exist on the islands," he shares of the inner islands. "To understand what it's like to hear the waves crashing against the rocks, to feel the salty sea breeze just under your nose, the ability to look out and see very far on the horizon, I think those are both very iconic. Then getting up to places like Cavern Point, Inspiration Point, and all the way out to Potato Harbor and Smugglers Cove, those are fantastic ways to spend a day at Santa Cruz Island. I think those two inner islands are really a great place to get exposed and for you to catch the island bug."

The full outer island experience requires longer boat rides, so it's better for longer camping trips.

TRAILBLAZING!

Island foxes are unique to the Channel Islands, inhabiting six of the eight islands and found nowhere else on Earth. They're the largest of the islands' native mammals, yet one of the smallest canid species in the world.

Views from the Channel Islands.

"Santa Rosa is an absolute island paradise with cloud forests, one of only two Torrey pine forests in the world. There's beautiful slot canyons, incredible biodiversity, pinnipeds, and clovers. Watching all these species in their natural environment makes you feel much more alone. Then you get out to San Miguel and you don't feel so alone because you're surrounded by potentially tens of thousands of pinnipeds. It's pretty amazing in little Santa Barbara, such an intimate experience. The cliffs are really majestic and you're likely going to be alone in enjoying the views."

Western

Joshua Tree National Park

ESTABLISHED	LOCATION
1994	Southern California
SIZE	VISITATION NO.
1,250 square miles	3,270,404
LAND ACKNOWLEDGMENT	Ancestral land of the Cahuilla, Mojave, Chemehuevi (Southern Paiute), Western Shoshone, and Serrano people
FOR MORE INFO, VISIT:	www.nps.gov/jotr

Often called the tree of the desert, Joshua trees are actually not trees, but a type of yucca plant with gnarled branches that, to some, resemble the biblical figure Joshua, guiding travelers westward. Joshua Tree National Park is made up of two distinct deserts—the Mojave and the Colorado—divided by the Pinto Basin Road. Each section has contrasting arid ecosystems influenced by their elevation. This desert park has something for everyone, be they hikers, climbers, campers, or tourists simply passing through. And that is Ranger Meg Rockwell's favorite thing about the park.

Ranger Meg's very first national park memory is visiting Denali National Park in Alaska. She traveled there by train and was greeted by a park ranger as she disembarked. She found herself wishing she had that fun job. Her path to becoming a park ranger began after she moved to Charleston, South Carolina, where she was surrounded by a number of National Park Service units. She was pursuing her bachelor's degree and started volunteering at Joshua Tree whenever she would make the trip out west.

During one of her college internships, she spent every weekend camping and volunteering at Congaree National Park, helping visitors with information, roving the park, and learning the different programs the park

Sunrise at the Cholla Cactus Garden can be a magical experience.

Joshua Tree National Park
California

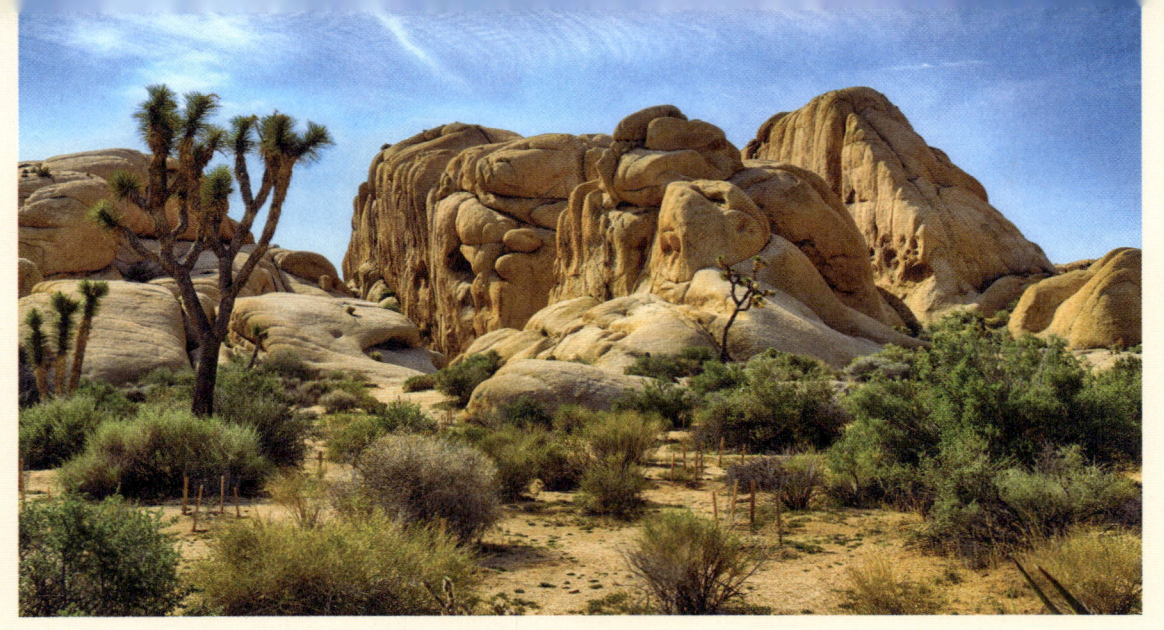

Joshua Tree is also home to large boulders made of monzogranite formations, once molten liquid heated by continuous movement of Earth's crust.

has to offer. After college, Ranger Meg applied to and got hired at Joshua Tree National Park. "When I visited places along the East Coast, it was their historical nature and the impacts these places had on this country that impressed me," she shares. "[But] it was the natural environments of the Wild West that most resonated with me. Joshua Tree National Park is one of my favorite places. I fell in love with the landscape almost immediately."

Ranger Meg enjoys talking to junior rangers about their park experiences and their favorite activity at the park (surprise, surprise, it's climbing on the rocks!). "National parks reach a wide audience. They are recognizable in our society for their important environmental messaging and mission of conservation, which aligns most closely with my own values," she says. "As a park ranger, I can talk to visitors about climate change and the effects it is having on the desert environment and ways we can do better. I enjoy making park visits fun, enjoyable, and no stress for visitors. I enjoy talking to visitors about ways they can enjoy the desert safely."

When you visit Joshua Tree National Park, Ranger Meg recommends that you enjoy any and all areas where nature inspires you. That could mean driving through the park and making stops along the way to check out wayside exhibitions at the designated pull-off areas or finding a spot at designated parking areas to hit the trail. If you're looking for picturesque views of Joshua trees and the monzogranite boulder formations, stay on the Mojave Desert (west) side of the park. For more cacti and wide-open landscapes as far as your eyes (and

> **TRAILBLAZING!**
>
> **The discovery of gold** in the Sierra Nevada foothills led miners to this area in the late 1860s. Desert Queen Mine, located within Joshua Tree, remained in operation until 1961, producing over 4,000 ounces of gold.

imagination) can see, the Colorado Desert (east) is the place to be. Sunrise at the Cholla Cactus Garden along the Pinto Basin Road is simply magical, and sunset along the Park Boulevard will offer you great views of the colorful desert landscape.

One thing to keep in mind if you enter the park from the south entrance: don't expect to see any Joshua trees for about 45 minutes, until you've reached the elevation that's conducive to the plant. As Ranger Meg describes it, "that means an enjoyable drive through a vast expanse of uninhabited desert surrounded by smoke trees, creosote, and other desert-native plants." Despite its vicinity to big cities like Los Angeles, San Diego, Palm Springs, and Las Vegas, Joshua Tree National Park still manages to offer a great amount of solitude and a magnificent night sky for Milky Way viewing and stargazing. Ranger Meg put it best: "It is a place where people can come for quiet and escape. It is grand and austere, and at the same time humbling to be in an environment that is millions of years old."

Joshua Tree National Park is one of the best places in Southern California to view the night sky.

Joshua Tree National Park
California

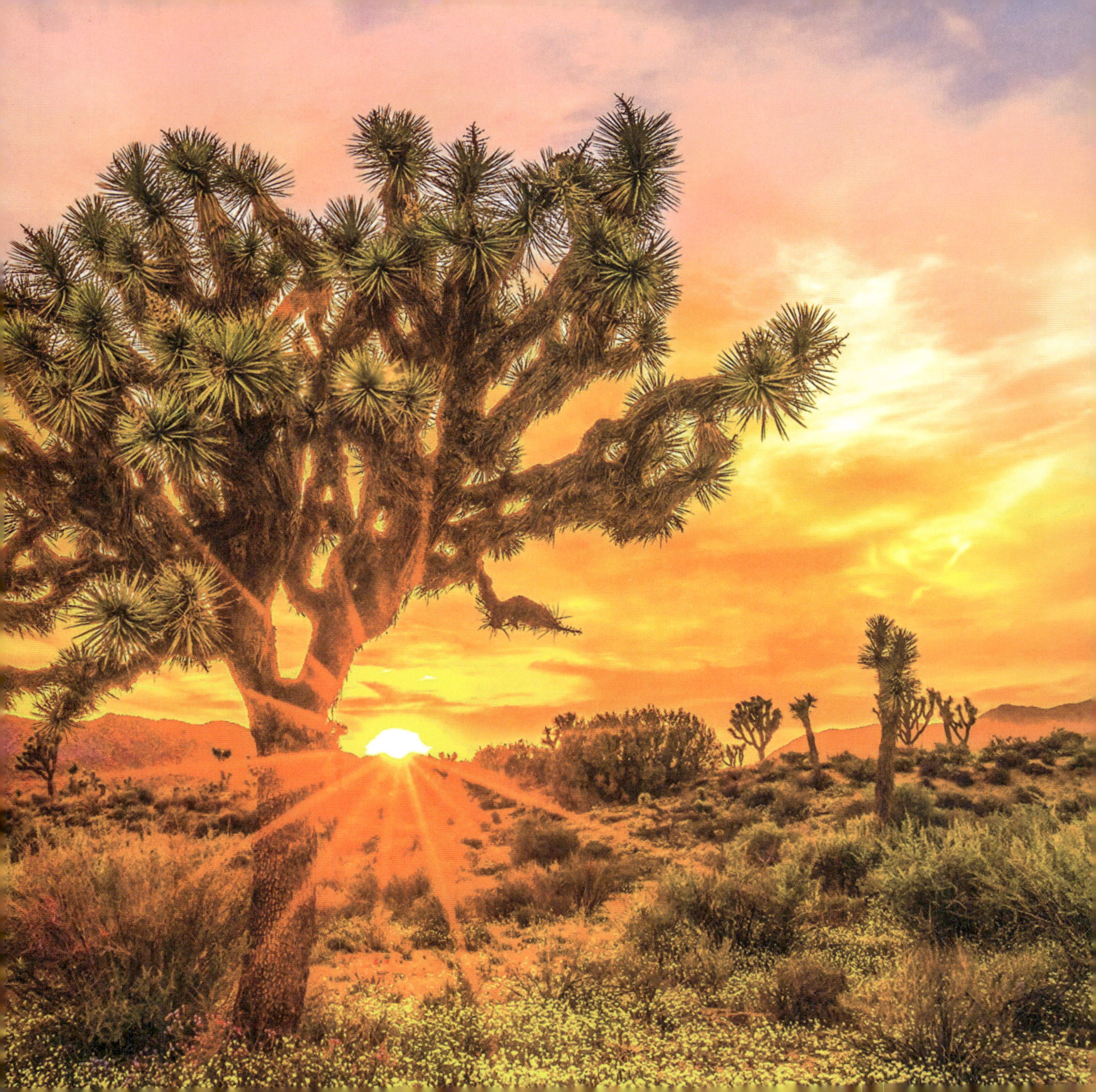

Western

Great Basin National Park

ESTABLISHED	LOCATION
1986	Eastern Nevada

SIZE	VISITATION NO.
121 square miles	143,265

LAND ACKNOWLEDGMENT
Ancestral land of the Western Shoshone, Goshute, Ute, Paiute, and Washoe people

FOR MORE INFO, VISIT:
www.nps.gov/grba

Ranger Bradley Mills' very first national park was Yosemite, when he was just a baby. Growing up in California, he was surrounded by a number of state and county parks, and his love for the outdoors became even more prominent during his university years, when he was supervising an outdoor adventures program. Motivated by a strong desire to adventure away from home and see more of the country, Bradley joined the US Forest Service before becoming a park ranger with the National Park Service.

Ranger Bradley is now the Lead Astronomer Ranger at Great Basin National Park, where he gets to spend time sharing the stellar night skies at the high desert park with visitors while directly participating in protecting our dark sky. "The number of people who come here having never seen the Milky Way, it fills me with joy being able to share that first experience with them," he says. "Certainly, an enormous motivator for being where I am is this night sky, and I wasn't dissimilar from folks who didn't get to see it at home. My first time was in the woods of Maine and I still remember vivid details from that moment. I just want to give that same awestruck feeling to anybody I can."

If you've had the opportunity to truly experience Great Basin National Park, you

Find alpine lakes in the high desert park, where the mountain peaks are rugged and the underground caverns are vast.

Fall colors in the Great Basin are stunning, with groves of aspen trees dotting the mountains in yellow, red, and gold.

might understand why it is a personal favorite of Ranger Bradley's. "I'm biased as a Great Basin National Park ranger, but I genuinely have found this to be one of my favorite parks," he shares. "The isolation, vast night skies, bristlecones, caves—you name it. This park has everything while being off the beaten path, which tends to bring more travelers who really care for the place since they had to put so much effort to reach here. I really enjoy . . . sharing my own love for this place, hoping it inspires some of their own."

When planning a visit to Great Basin, Ranger Bradley advises that you prepare for isolation and make several backup plans. Since the park is fairly remote, it's a good idea to have a full tank of gas and to ensure your car battery is in good condition. Though the park isn't necessarily crowded most of the time, find even more solitude (and great trails and views) down the gravel road to Snake Creek or Strawberry Creek. Great Basin National Park ranges in elevation from 6,825 feet to 13,065 feet above sea level between its highest and lowest trails, so there might be road closures due to snow in the winter, coupled with below-freezing temperatures. Either plan for these conditions or visit during the summer.

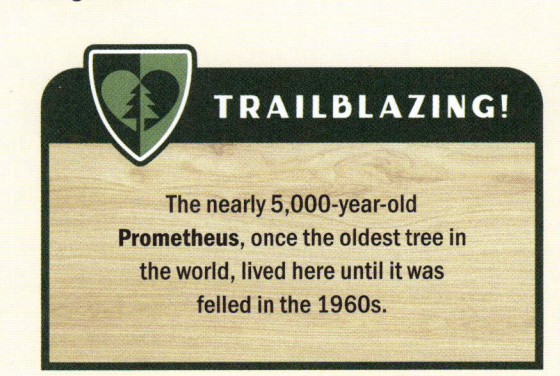

TRAILBLAZING!

The nearly 5,000-year-old **Prometheus**, once the oldest tree in the world, lived here until it was felled in the 1960s.

Western

Grand Canyon National Park

Carved predominantly by the Colorado River and rising thousands of feet above sea level, the Grand Canyon is a magnificent sight. Spanning the northern Arizona desert, the canyon is often measured by following the path of the river, at 277 miles long, up to 18 miles wide, and 1 mile deep—so massive that it is visible from space!

Cheyenne Yanez grew up in southern California. Her very first national park trip, with her husband Vic Robledo and their young daughter Penny, was a grand one. "Grand Canyon was a very popular choice at the time," she says. "We decided to go there for the first time spontaneously in 2015 during our week off from work on a day trip from Los Angeles, not knowing what to expect. It was a summer day in July and we spent the entire day at the park. We were in awe and mesmerized by its picture-perfect, jaw-dropping panoramic scene. We enjoyed the sunset before driving back home the same night. When we realized our entrance park pass was valid for seven days, we bought camping gear and headed straight back to the Grand Canyon four days later to camp for the very first time. That's when our obsession for national parks began."

The Colorado River runs 277 miles through the Grand Canyon.

ESTABLISHED	LOCATION
1919	Northern Arizona
SIZE	**VISITATION NO.**
1,902 square miles	4,733,705
LAND ACKNOWLEDGMENT	Ancestral land of the Diné (Navajo), Havasupai, Hualapai, Hopi, Yavapai-Apache, Kaibab, Southern Paiute, and Zuni people
FOR MORE INFO, VISIT:	www.nps.gov/grca

River rafting down the Colorado River gives you unique perspectives of the scale and magnitude of the canyon.

Sarah Olzawski is a national park lover I met through outdoor communities. We connected over her desire to travel solo to some of these remote places. The first national park to which she traveled solo was the Grand Canyon. "My first glimpse of the Grand Canyon will stay with me for the rest of my life," she recalls. "I got there really early and there were hardly any other people there yet. The sun had just come up and, since it was March, there were still some frosty areas in the canyon. There is no way to describe your first view of the Grand Canyon without sounding totally cliche. Awe-inspiring doesn't even capture it. As a Cherokee citizen, I immediately noticed that this park names the people who were the original inhabitants of the land, on a seal near the rim. It was so quiet and serene before the crowds showed up, and I really took my time taking in the view."

Sarah chose to make her bucket-list journey about the national parks because they're so iconic and part of the fabric of the US's history. "This land is where history happened. As an Indigenous person, I make it a point to learn about the Indigenous Peoples who originally called our parks home, and I always investigate to see if the parks are doing a good job of including Indigenous

Grand Canyon National Park
Arizona

> **TRAILBLAZING!**
>
> The Hopi tribe believe that **Sipapuni**, a travertine dome made of limestone located at the confluence of the Colorado and Little Colorado Rivers, is the place of emergence. Upon death, a person passes through this point on their journey to the afterlife.

history and perspectives in their visitor centers and exhibits," Sarah says. "I also love national parks because they are international destinations. People from all over the world visit our parks, and I love talking to and learning from the other visitors I encounter there."

Ranger Joelle Baird's first visit to a National Park Service unit was during a visit to Washington, DC, as a young kid, before she even knew that the National Mall was part of the National Park Service. She later interned with the Student Conservation Association—a non-profit organization that provides hands-on environmental conservation programs for youth and young adults—as part of their trail crew. That experience took her to her first big national park, Denali. Today, Ranger Jo has been at the Grand Canyon National Park for over a decade in a variety of roles. "I'm still blown away by the landscape and especially when having friends or family visit or even observing new visitors who come to see the Grand Canyon for the first time," she says. "You can see it through their eyes, just how remarkable and unique this place is."

During her free time, Ranger Jo enjoys hiking in the inner canyon, especially the trails that are off the beaten path. Morning hikes are the best to avoid peak heat and crowds. She also loves the Desert View viewpoint located at the end of Desert View Road. "It's a little different than when you go to the Grand Canyon Village area. You can really see a lot of the Colorado River from that vantage point, and the painted desert as well," she shares. "That landscape, where you get a chance to see the Canyon and the Colorado River at the same time, that's the money shot right there. The view from the watchtower itself is a good one." I'm inclined to agree.

One pro tip from Ranger Jo is to spend the night at the park, if you have the time and resources, so you can really take in the landscape and not rush from one viewpoint to another. "We do have a lot of visitors who just drive up here off the interstate and they only have a couple hours to see the canyon, and that's great, but to truly get to know the canyon and appreciate it even more, I think folks just have to spend more time here," she says. "We do have a lot of accommodation in the park as well as immediately outside the park boundaries in our gateway community of Tusayan. So if people do have a little more time, it's definitely worthwhile to spend a night or two here to get to know more about the canyon, its history, and the great resources that we have here."

The Desert View Watchtower was constructed in 1932. It was designed by architect Mary Colter, who was influenced by the architecture of the Ancestral Puebloan people of the Colorado Plateau.

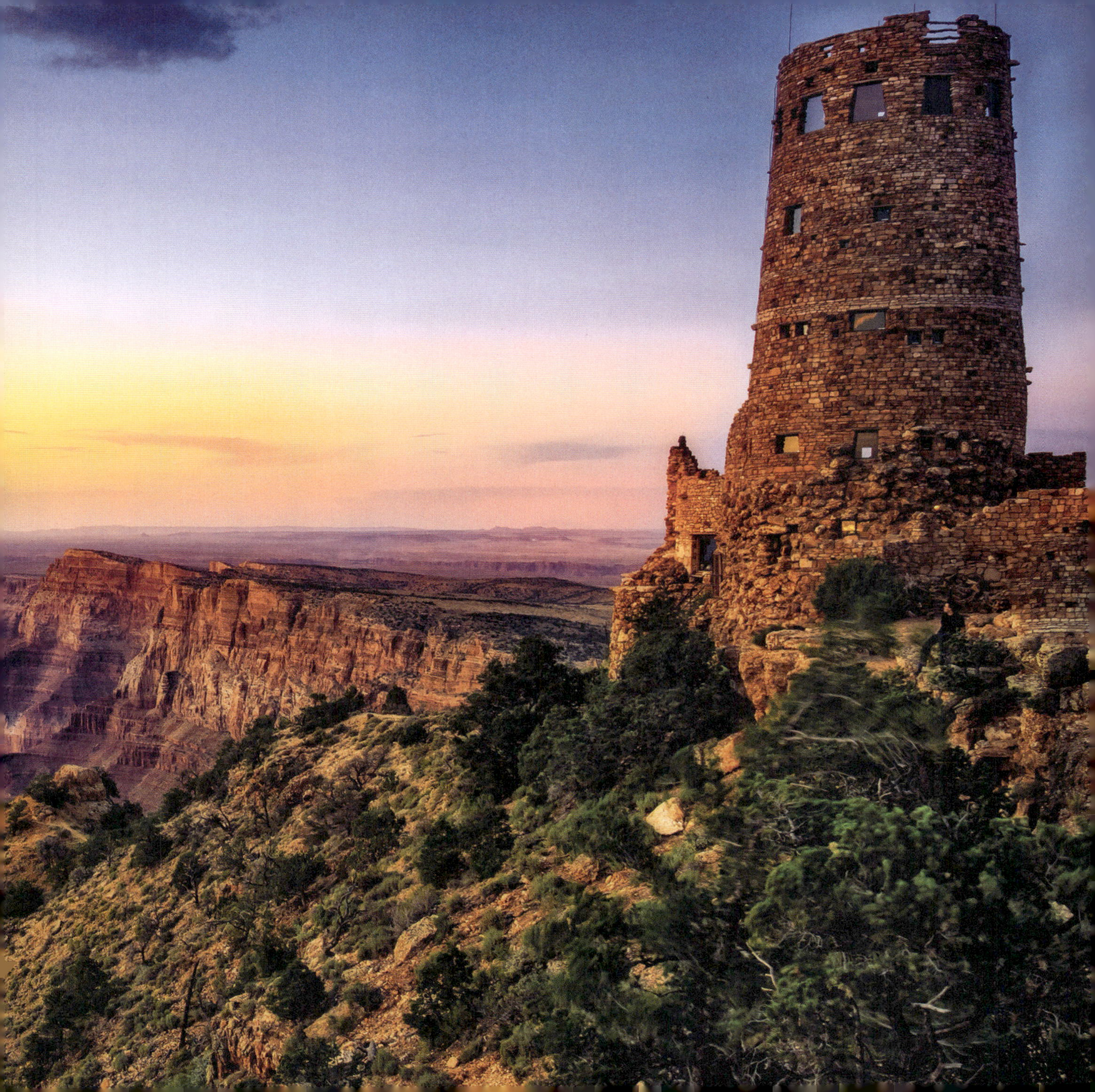

Western

Petrified Forest National Park

ESTABLISHED	LOCATION
1962	Northeastern Arizona
SIZE	VISITATION NO.
346 square miles	520,491

LAND ACKNOWLEDGMENT

Ancestral land of the Zuni, Pueblo, Hopi Tutskwa, and Diné Bikéyah (Navajo) people

FOR MORE INFO, VISIT:

www.nps.gov/pefo

The only things that are petrifying about Petrified Forest National Park are the trees. Though it's often labeled as a "drive-through" park due its location—conveniently situated off Interstate 40—this park is rich in history, dating back more than 200 million years. As a geology nut and rock lover, this park hits the jackpot for my desert-dwelling self. The crystallized minerals in the woods, the colorful painted dunes, and the purple-hued badlands form a beautiful and unique landscape.

For Ranger Sarah Herve, a nature-loving kid who grew up admiring her older brother's role as a park ranger at Point Reyes National Seashore in California, this park is fascinating because researchers from all over the world flock there to study the fossils.

There's never a single story to be told, as new discoveries are constantly being made, and that makes Ranger Sarah's job as Chief of Interpretation a fun one. "I love the paleontology aspect of the park," she shares. "The science that's happening is really cool, but we also have multiple stories in this park. We have an incredible archaeological history of westward expansion via Route 66, which runs through the park, so we have an opportunity to connect with people on modern American history perspectives. And then there's the geology. If

Hike amongst the bluish bentonite clay badland hills on the Blue Mesa Trail.

The petrified woods in this park date back almost 225 million years, preserving fossils from the Late Triassic period.

it wasn't for the geology, we wouldn't have all the cool fossils that we have here today." Ranger Sarah loves talking to park visitors about the park's rock formations, the red part of the painted desert, how things happened geologically, and about the namesake of the park.

Petrified Forest was one of the first national parks established in the early 1900s, and it maintains a varied and impressive ecology. Pronghorn, elk deer, coyotes, bobcats, and roadrunners are just some of the animals you can see roaming in the park. Another important piece of this park is its human history. "We have amazing rock art in the park," Ranger Sarah says. "We live in a place that the first peoples of our nation call home. We have petroglyphs and other evidence of Ancestral Puebloan cultures. Those people, their descendants, are still here, and we work alongside them. You don't get to have that everywhere in the country, so that's something that I've really grown to deeply appreciate, and I've learned about different cultures of people that lived here before colonialism."

The first thing Ranger Sarah recommends doing before visiting is checking the park's website for the most current opening hours, as the park gates are locked in the evening. She also recommends that people get on a trail to see the petrified woods and immerse themselves in an area surrounded by these geological treasures. The park has a demonstration fossil lab, where visitors can watch paleontologists cleaning and examining newly found fossils. In terms of trail recommendations, Ranger Sarah loves the Jasper Forest. Other trails I personally love and recommend would be the Crystal Forest, Blue Mesa, and Giant Log trails.

TRAILBLAZING!

The largest concentration of **petroglyphs** in the park can be found at Newspaper Rock, where more than 650 individual markings can be seen. They were created by the Puebloan people between 650 and 2,000 years ago.

Western

Saguaro National Park

Saguaro National Park is home to the largest concentration of saguaro cacti, the largest cactus species in the United States. Saguaro cacti are only found in the Sonoran Desert. Tucson, Arizona, divides the park into the East (Rincon Mountain) and West (Tucson Mountain) districts. The views here are iconic, like something out of old movies about the Wild West.

Born to migrant farmworker parents in Yuma, Arizona, and later growing up in Fresno, California, Ranger Cam Juárez's first national park was Yosemite.

ESTABLISHED	LOCATION
1994	Southern Arizona
SIZE	**VISITATION NO.**
143 square miles	1,010,906
LAND ACKNOWLEDGMENT	Ancestral land of the Akimel O'odham (Pima), Apache, Hopi, Maricopa, Yaqui, Tohono O'odham (Desert People), Yavapai, and Zuni people
FOR MORE INFO, VISIT:	www.nps.gov/sagu

Saguaro are generally considered to be "adult" at approximately 125 years of age.

His family traveled back and forth between California and Arizona, following the agriculture crops, before he settled down in Tucson. Living in Arizona, Ranger Cam was no stranger to Grand Canyon and Petrified Forest National Parks, but it took him sitting on a panel with the then Superintendent of Saguaro National Park for him to realize that there was a national park right in his city.

Having grown up as an activist, Ranger Cam is passionate about the environment, conservation, and representation, focusing on their impact on people. After his very first visit to Saguaro National Park, his career with the National Park Service began in 2016, when he became the park's first Community Engagement and Outreach Coordinator. As a park ranger, he is always intentional about his work, prioritizing diversity, representation, and recreation for people of color, while honoring and working alongside the Indigenous People in the area.

"I think the biggest problem we have is deferred storytelling," Ranger Cam says. "We talk constantly about telling America's stories, but I think we only tell a certain number of stories. I regularly remind park rangers who consider themselves to be American storytellers of the African proverb, 'Until the lion learns how to write, every story will glorify the hunter.' I'm proud to be an American and I'm also a political thinker. In the last few years, our national parks have allowed us to tell those stories in a way that is inclusive and respectful."

The Tohono O'odham, the tribal community, call the saguaros "ha:san" (pronounced hashan), which means people. "In their traditional ways, they see the ha:san as an embodiment of the spirit of their ancestors that have passed on versus going to heaven," Ranger

The park has two scenic drives: the Cactus Forest Loop in the Rincon Mountain District (east) and the Bajada Loop in the Tucson Mountain District (west).

TRAILBLAZING!

Saguaro is home to **Gila monsters**, one of the two venomous lizards on Earth. Each Gila lizard has a unique pattern, similar to how fingerprints are unique to each human on Earth.

Cam explains. "So when you visit Saguaro West District and see two million saguaros there, it's like their entire lineage is standing there in the sun."

Ranger Cam's favorite season at Saguaro National Park is, believe it or not, the hottest time of the year. One of the special occasions that takes place at the park in early summer is the harvesting of saguaro fruit, called "bahidaj" by the Tohono O'odham. "There's a huge focus on the tribal community because they have a lot going on during their new year," he says. "They harvest the fruit in the parks and we do a lot of education around that. I started a program called the Red Hill Speaker series to provide the opportunity to tell everyone's stories. We invite underrepresented communities to talk about their connection to the land. We're really intentional about getting those communities there first, and ever since being implemented, we've seen more diversity in our audiences in our special programs."

There are fewer saguaros in the East District because of cattle-grazing activities there prior to 1978,

The Tohono O'odham call the saguaros "ha:san," an embodiment of the spirit of their ancestors that have passed on.

so Ranger Cam suggests doing more wilderness hiking on that side. For Instagram-worthy saguaros, the west side is best. He recommends that visitors make time to go to both sides of the park and see the differences in landscapes and activities. "Saguaro National Park is not just about the saguaro plant," he says. "It's about so many other species. Saguaro itself is a keystone species, but at various times of the year we have different things going on, like the saguaro fruit harvest in the summer, the monarch butterfly migration in the fall. It's amazing to see that happen."

Ranger Cam's favorite trail on the west side is Signal Hills, which showcases the largest petroglyph site in the Tucson Mountain District. The trail also connects to Wasson Peak for a longer day-hike, where you'll be treated to expansive views of the park and the city of Tucson. Loma Verde Loop is another one of Ranger Cam's favorite trails on the east side. Whichever trail you choose for your adventure, be sure to bring plenty of water, even in winter.

Ranger Cam says of his job, "I love the work that I'm doing and I love that I'm able to create a space for other people of color to come in and grow and do the things that are important to do for our communities." If you live locally, Ranger Cam invites you to volunteer at the park so you can truly understand things like why buffelgrass is an invasive species and such a threat to the ecosystem. Speaking from my personal experience volunteering at national park sites, you will indeed have a different appreciation for the park.

Saquaro National Park
Arizona

Western

Haleakalā National Park

Legend has it that, on the summit of this giant shield volcano, the demigod Maui snared the sun from its journey across the sky, only releasing it upon the sun's promise to slow its descent and make the day last longer. In fact, Haleakalā means "house of the sun." Haleakalā National Park extends from the mountains at the Summit District to the sea at the coastal Kīpahulu District.

The park and the island of Maui are also home to Ranger Honeygirl Duman, who first visited Haleakalā on a second-grade field trip. She remembers watching her bag of chips expand as the school bus climbed alongside the dormant volcano, on the way to the Haleakalā summit. The natural progression for many high schoolers in Hawai'i upon graduation is to work in the tourism industry. And so she did, for 17 years, before going back to school to learn more about her Hawaiian heritage. She recalls, "I really felt like I needed to do something for my people, for my land, for my island." She has a passion for Hawaiian language—inspired by her grandmother, who speaks the language—and is also a total botany geek. With this background, Ranger

Hike along the Pipiwai Trail in the Kīpahulu District and listen to the bamboo leaves rattle and the stalks creak, clack, and pop.

ESTABLISHED	LOCATION
1961	East Maui, Hawai'i
SIZE	**VISITATION NO.**
52 square miles	791,292
LAND ACKNOWLEDGMENT	
Ancestral land of the Native Hawaiians and the Polynesians from the Marquesas Islands	
FOR MORE INFO, VISIT:	
www.nps.gov/hale	

Honeygirl went on to become a park ranger at Haleakalā National Park.

Working at the park is more than just a job for Ranger Honeygirl, a true native of the Hawaiian islands, it is a lifestyle, a way of thinking, and a way to connect with the land that she's rooted in. "When I see students or interns that I worked with eventually get hired in the park, that brings me the most joy," she shares. "That is why I do what I do. My brain might be so tired some days or I might get frustrated because it's not working today, but when I see the end results, the engagement that I have with students or with the park resources, and then connecting with them when they tell me 'my brother planted that plant over there' or 'I can't wait to come up next time to learn more about the park,' that definitely brings me the most joy."

Ranger Honeygirl suggests the Hosmer Grove Loop trail at Haleakalā because "it's the easiest place you can go and see our Hawaiian forest birds while we still have them. It's a great contrast between the intended conservation act of introducing non-native species to what it's supposed to look like. I love that contrast." She also suggests the Kalahaku Overlook. "Not many people access that overlook," she says, "but when you look down, it's very peaceful. Sometimes you have clouds moving in and out. You can see inside the crater and I think it's a place where people just pass by without even stopping for a few moments."

The Haleakalā summit was once 5,000 feet higher than it is today. The massive valley was carved by water and landslides.

At Haleakalā, you can learn about which seabirds or geese that nest at different times of the year, and which bird is sipping nectar from which plant. Ranger Honeygirl invites visitors to the park and the islands of Hawai'i to learn about the land, its people, and their culture before their trip. Take the time to learn what makes Hawai'i Hawai'i, and about the people who lived on the islands before colonization.

TRAILBLAZING!

Only **5 percent** of this shield volcano is above sea level. When measured from base (ocean floor) to summit, Haleakalā is 28,000 feet tall. It's believed that the summit once surpassed the height of Mount Everest, before erosion took its toll.

Western

Hawai'i Volcanoes National Park

Sacred, diverse, dynamic, and, as the name suggests, very volcanic, Hawai'i Volcanoes National Park is a must-see for national park lovers. Pele, the Hawaiian volcano deity, is said to have created the volcanic landscapes seen today in this national park. As the two shield volcanoes in the park, Kilauea and Mauna Loa, go through the stop and start cycles of active eruptions, Pele's spirit can be felt by those who visit her volcanic domain.

Working at Hawai'i Volcanoes National Park is a dream job for Ranger Jessica Ferracane. She first moved to Hawai'i when she was 12 years old, but only remembers visiting the park as an adult. She was a journalist and went to Hawai'i Volcanoes on assignment, to capture the sights and excitement of an ongoing eruption, with lava flowing into the ocean, for a guidebook. "The park ranger shared some of the trails to see the rainforest, and I was hooked," she shares. "Years later, I returned to the park, but this time, as an emergency hire during the eruption in 2011. The park's Public Information Officer had recently retired and they needed help managing all the media. It was divine providence."

Ranger Jessica loves that no two days are ever the same at Hawai'i Volcanoes. With the island itself made up of six individual volcanoes combined, the land is ever-changing. "In 2018, Kilauea had a massive summit collapse when the magma chamber drained out and all the lava went into the East Rift zone," she says. "That closed the park for 134 days. We've had a couple of reactions in the summit crater of Kilauea since then and each one is different. Part of the road around Kilauea Caldera on the Crater Rim Drive dropped into the caldera in 2018. So we go through these staggering changes occasionally, which alter the landscape. I don't know any other national park that is like that. That constant change and uncertainty, that's like my mental coffee going into work."

For a park as dynamic as Hawai'i Volcanoes, Ranger Jessica stresses the importance of visiting the park's website to get the latest updates. Another important

ESTABLISHED	LOCATION
1916	Hawai'i Island, Hawai'i
SIZE	**VISITATION NO.**
523 square miles (and counting!)	1,620,294
LAND ACKNOWLEDGMENT	
Ancestral land of the Native Hawaiians and the Polynesians from the Marquesas Islands	
FOR MORE INFO, VISIT:	
www.nps.gov/havo	

The Hōlei Sea Arch in Hawai'i Volcanoes.

aspect of trip planning is to remain flexible and manage your expectations. "There might not be parking at a certain place, but there's so much more to explore," she assures. "This park is huge, stretching from sea level all the way to the almost 14,000-foot summit of Mauna Loa. Try to explore the areas that are off the beaten path. To me, that's where you really connect with Hawai'i Volcanoes National Park."

One of Ranger Jessica's favorite trails is called the Kīpukapuaulu Trail, a 1.2-mile loop with gentle inclines and declines. "It goes through a part of the park that has been protected from cattle, goats, and sheep grazing because they eat everything, destroying the forest," she explains. "This part of the park has been protected since the '70s and you can actually get into a forest that is much like it was precontact, before anybody got to the Hawaiian Islands." Another spot that we both agree on is the Kahuku Unit on the western end of Big Island, for the charm and solitude it provides. "No matter how busy it is at Kilauea, you can find solace and solitude at the Kahuku unit because it's definitely lesser-known. The trails there are wonderful," she says. "It's also a great place to have a picnic and talk to rangers about what that landscape used to be like."

My first time experiencing Hawai'i Volcanoes National Park, in 2017, was pure magic. The Kilauea caldera was active, with lava flowing through lava tubes into the ocean. One of the recommended viewing spots is the town of Kalapana, a village destroyed and covered in 80 feet of Pāhoehoe lava rocks during a massive

Hawai'i Volcanoes National Park
Hawai'i

> **TRAILBLAZING!**
>
> Hawai'i Volcanoes has both the most active volcano, **Kīlauea**, and the largest active volcano on Earth, **Mauna Loa**. Mauna Loa makes up roughly half of island of Hawai'i and, from the ocean floor, stands 30,000 feet tall, taller than Mount Everest.

eruption in 1986. When I visited, my national park adventure buddy, Mary, and I biked the six miles to get to the viewing area. I was totally mesmerized by the flow of lava draining into the ocean. The orange of the lava glowing brighter as the horizon darkened. It was truly a once-in-a-lifetime opportunity, since eruptions are so unpredictable and there's no guarantee that lava will flow into the ocean every time.

I was very fortunate to return to the park in early 2023. This time, I took my husband and my mother-in-law to experience the power of Pele. The timing was great as the Kilauea summit was actively erupting. We stayed in Hilo, making the trip to Hawai'i Volcanoes just a quick 40-minute drive. Our first day there was spent hiking the one-mile trek to Keanakāko'i Overlook an hour before sunrise. My husband, Karey, says, "The trail was slightly uphill, damp, and muggy. A headlamp was useful in the dark for the 20 minute hike to what I nicknamed Madame Pele's performance. The volcano was nothing short of sublime, almost medicinal the longer I gazed at the lava fountain. Exploding and volatile, yet centered, majestic at the same time. She danced on her stage of volcanic rock formations, and trees that fluttered as percussions; ivory ribbons of smoke waved like wind balloons swaying, drawing our attention to Madame Pele who discoed, bopped, and rock and rolled nonstop for her audience of tourists, scientists, photographers, and anyone not expecting to be so lucky in seeing this rare phenomenon. It was, in a word, arresting . . . "

We still talk about the trip. For him, it was a life-changing experience.

A rare sighting of lava flowing into the ocean during a volcano eruption at Hawai'i Volcanoes National Park.

Western

National Park of American Samoa

ESTABLISHED	LOCATION
1988	American Samoa

SIZE	VISITATION NO.
21 square miles	12,135

LAND ACKNOWLEDGMENT
Ancestral land of the Indigenous Samoans of Polynesians ancestry

FOR MORE INFO, VISIT:
www.nps.gov/npsa

More than just a national park, the National Park of American Samoa is indeed a tropical paradise. Aside from the planning process, getting to the park itself is the other half of the battle. But once there, you won't want to leave.

Considering how unique this national park is, I was privileged to connect with Anthony Wyberski, who grew up in American Samoa. It's no surprise that his first national park was the one he now works in today. His best memories from the park are times spent doing field work and going off trails with the crew in search of invasive species. "Every day was a new location and seeing more of the forest and possible ancient sites of my ancestors," he shares. "Getting lost in the forest will never get old to me. Just knowing that my ancestors walked these lands and I get the chance to follow them, it's special."

Looking for an alternative to college so he could help support his family, Ranger Anthony landed a seasonal position at the national park. Working there, he grew to understand the mission of the National Park Service—a common goal of stewardship and preservation—which also became his passion. A few years later, he applied for a permanent position with the park and became the Maintenance Supervisor for the National Park of American Samoa.

Ranger Anthony encourages visitors to stop by the visitor center and connect with the rangers. It's a great opportunity to learn not just about the park and the landscape, but also about the people and the local culture. "And when you go hiking, take it all in and look around," he adds. "The culture is all around you."

The National Park of American Samoa was the most difficult park for me to plan to visit, even more difficult than the eight Alaskan national parks combined! It also didn't help that I'm not an American citizen, which meant more challenges (and extra paperwork). There were few resources available at the time to help me plan for my trip, but I knew a friend from Instagram who had visited and who could offer tips and recommendations.

Meet Christa Eileen from south Louisiana. Christa loves making lists and setting attainable goals and, like others in this book, she set out to visit all 63 national parks. One year, around Christmas, she journeyed to American Samoa with two of her hiking friends. "We arrived late in Pago Pago and made Sadie's by the Sea our home base for a few days. I recommend this place because it's situated on the water, very laid back, has a restaurant with great drinks, food, and, above all else, a great view! From Sadie's, it's a quick 15-minute walk to the park's visitor center. Ask for Ranger Ronald when you're there. He has a wealth of knowledge and will introduce you to all the wonderful things that the Samoan culture has to offer. We didn't know it at the time, but he was setting up our trip to become one for the record books when he connected us to Peter, a Samoan chief who gave us an authentic Samoan experience on the island when he hosted us over in his village."

For most visitors, their visit to the National Park of American Samoa centers around the town of Pago Pago

TRAILBLAZING!

In American Samoa, land ownership is communal by the **'âiga (cognatic descent groups)**, so there are no federally owned lands. The National Park Service is currently leasing the land from native villages and the American Samoa government as part of a 50-year lease agreement.

Located south of the equator, National Park of American Samoa boasts a tropical climate which is predominantly warm, humid, and rainy year-round.

on Tutuila Island. This is where commercial planes land and cruise ships dock. But for those who venture away from Pago Pago to the other two islands of Ta'ū, and Ofu, paradise awaits. And that's exactly what Christa and her friends did. Before heading out of Pago Pago, they squeezed in a couple of hikes on Tutuila Island, including Lower Sauma Ridge, which leads down to astounding

National Park of American Samoa
American Samoa

blue pools; Tuafanua Trail for the rainforests, rocky beaches, and ladders; and Pola Island Trail for a stroll down to yet another rocky beach.

"We took a plane to Ta'ū then hopped directly into the back of a truck, which then took us to the boat harbor," Christa says. "After getting to the harbor, we hopped onto another boat for about 15 miles in the Pacific Ocean to the island of Ofu. My friends and I were all powering through this extremely rough boat ride. Once our seasick boat ride was over, we got into the back of another pickup truck. The truck then drove us to Va'oto Lodge, our home for the remainder of the trip. The owner of the lodge, Deb, is truly a blessing. She included us in a lot of the daily activities that she did around the lodge, from cooking to running errands, and even Christmas celebrations. If you're staying with Deb, be sure to ask her about the coconut crabs that live on land and can be found at night. These are such a delicacy and a must-try while on island.

"Is the trip out to Ofu worth it? Yes! If you're looking to relax and truly enjoy the tranquility of the Samoan Islands, the trip out to Ofu is well worth it. If you stay with Deb at Va'oto, you can ride bikes and do some exploring on your own. If you're ready to hit the beach, pack a bag with a great book (maybe a national park book), snacks, and drinks, and head down to Ofu Beach. This is the iconic view of American Samoa and is one not to be missed! I would plan on spending at least three hours there. We loved it so much, this is where we spent our Christmas morning."

Rocky Mountain National Park
Colorado

Rocky Mountain

The Rocky Mountain region is full of mile-high wonders, including mountain ranges that are still actively forming, colorful badlands, red rocks, thermal hot spots, and well-preserved cultural sites of the Ancestral Puebloans. Filled with diverse landscapes and even more diverse wildlife inhabiting the land, air, and water, this region is home to some large mammals, like grizzly bears, moose, elk, mule deer, and, yes, even the elusive wolves. Although the number of mountain-related superlatives is off the charts in this region, it can be surprising to learn that the highest concentration of natural sandstone arches in the world can also be found here, in Utah, as well as the two tallest dunes in North America, which are in Colorado. Some of the parks here are on the popular list for visitation, and some are less-mentioned gems that deserve to be highlighted.

Rocky Mountain
Glacier National Park

Named for its namesake remnants of glaciers from the ice age, this "Crown of the Continent" park is home to 25 glaciers that are actively thawing and melting. The landscapes at Glacier National Park have been shaped by glacial forces over the last 2 million years, resulting in large U-shaped valleys and rugged topography.

As a kid who grew up in Marin County, California, Doug Mitchell had the opportunity to experience both Muir Woods National Monument and Point Reyes National Seashore. Doug shares, "Like many kids of my generation, my passion for the natural world was kindled by an extraordinary educator. In my case, that educator was the amazing Mrs. Elizabeth Terwilliger. Her advocacy and commitment to education made her a legend, and I still visit Terwilliger Grove in Muir Woods when I get back to Marin County."

Today, Doug serves as the Executive Director at Glacier National Park Conservancy, a non-profit friend organization that supports the park. "When I think of national parks, I think of family," he says. "My wife Julie grew up here in Glacier Country, and many of our most special family memories have taken place both here in Glacier and in other treasured public lands. And when I say 'family' I use that term in its many forms. Julie and I have had special times just the two of us (we always celebrate our anniversary—40 of them now—with a hike). We've had important connective experiences with our two

Mountain goats are exceptional climbers and are often found traversing nearly vertical cliffs.

ESTABLISHED	LOCATION
1910	Northwestern Montana
SIZE	**VISITATION NO.**
1,583 square miles	2,933,616
LAND ACKNOWLEDGMENT	
Ancestral land of the Blackfeet, Salish, Pend d'Oreille, and Kootenai people	
FOR MORE INFO, VISIT:	
www.nps.gov/glac	

View of Wild Goose Island on Saint Mary Lake, the second largest lake in Glacier National Park.

boys and now with their wives, and we've had broader 'family' experiences with her side of the family and mine."

While Glacier will always be Doug's favorite park, he's hoping that even in his 60s, he will continue to discover new places and experience other national parks. "Like President Franklin Roosevelt famously said, 'There is nothing so American as our national parks,'" he says. "The scenery and the wildlife are native. The fundamental idea behind the parks is native. It is, in brief, that the country belongs to the people." That sense of connection to the land resonates with me and makes me feel that these places are an important part of who we are as people and that allow us access to a space that helps us be our best selves."

National park lover Amanda Bauler also calls Glacier a family favorite. "I'm a mountain person, and I just can't think of anything more glorious than a day hiking to glacier-fed lakes surrounded by snow-capped peaks," she says. "My husband is a wildlife photographer, so the abundant wildlife and spectacular mountain views make this park especially appealing. This park also holds great memories for us. We hiked the 14-mile Highline Trail with our three older girls when our youngest was seven. It was our toughest hike together as a family, but the views were just so worth it! And for a little added excitement we almost missed the last

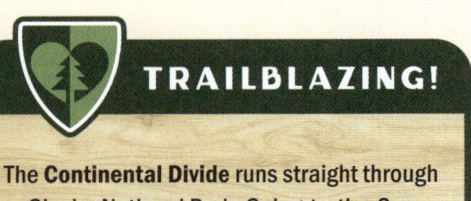

TRAILBLAZING!

The **Continental Divide** runs straight through Glacier National Park. Going-to-the-Sun Road, the only road that goes across the park, crosses the divide at Logan Pass.

shuttle of the day to return us to the parking area where we had left our car."

For Sarah Olzawski, a fellow national park lover, participating in her first-ever guided group hike with the Glacier Institute was a safe way to experience the bear country. "As a solo traveler and hiker, I didn't know what to expect, but I ended up having the perfect day in the lesser-known Two Medicine area of the park. Our guide on the hike was amazing, telling us all about the various plants we passed and about the geology of the area. I had such a good time, I'll definitely be doing more guided hikes in the future." Glacier is also her favorite of the big parks so far, for its vast diversity of ecosystems: "I wasn't expecting to see such different landscapes at Glacier."

Chris Zayas and her national-park-loving family arrived at Glacier National Park the day before the Going-to-the-Sun Road opened up for the season. "They were still digging out of 90-foot snow drifts! There's never enough time to see these parks and this was no different. We saw so much, but there was so much left to see. Even if you never step foot out of the car, the views from the road are stunning and the hairpin turns and drop-offs take your breath away. I do highly recommend

The Highline Trail is one of the most popular hikes in the park. It's not for the faint of heart, but the views are rewarding.

over to Grandma Joy and sat down beside her, wanting to share her binoculars with Grandma Joy. Although they were separated by eight decades in age and even with a language barrier, it was that magic of nature, the spectacle of seeing the moose in this beautiful national park, that brought them together and allowed them to share this moment of joy. The national parks have a way of creating that space where we can all come together through that mutual love and reverence for the beauty of the great outdoors."

The Redrock Falls are found along the Swiftcurrent Pass Trail.

stepping foot out of your car every chance you get, though, because the natural beauty of the park is stupendous."

Another national-park-loving duo, Brad Ryan and his grandmother, Joy Ryan, remember the moments driving up Going-to-the-Sun Road and hiking along the Continental Divide Trail heading to Fishercap Lake to watch moose grazing at dusk. "There was a little girl who was probably about four years old, from Eastern Europe," Brad remembers. "She did not speak English and she was wearing a polka-dotted pair of tights and a polka-dotted fleece that matched Grandma Joy's. She walked

Wildflowers blooming in summer.

Glacier National Park
Montana

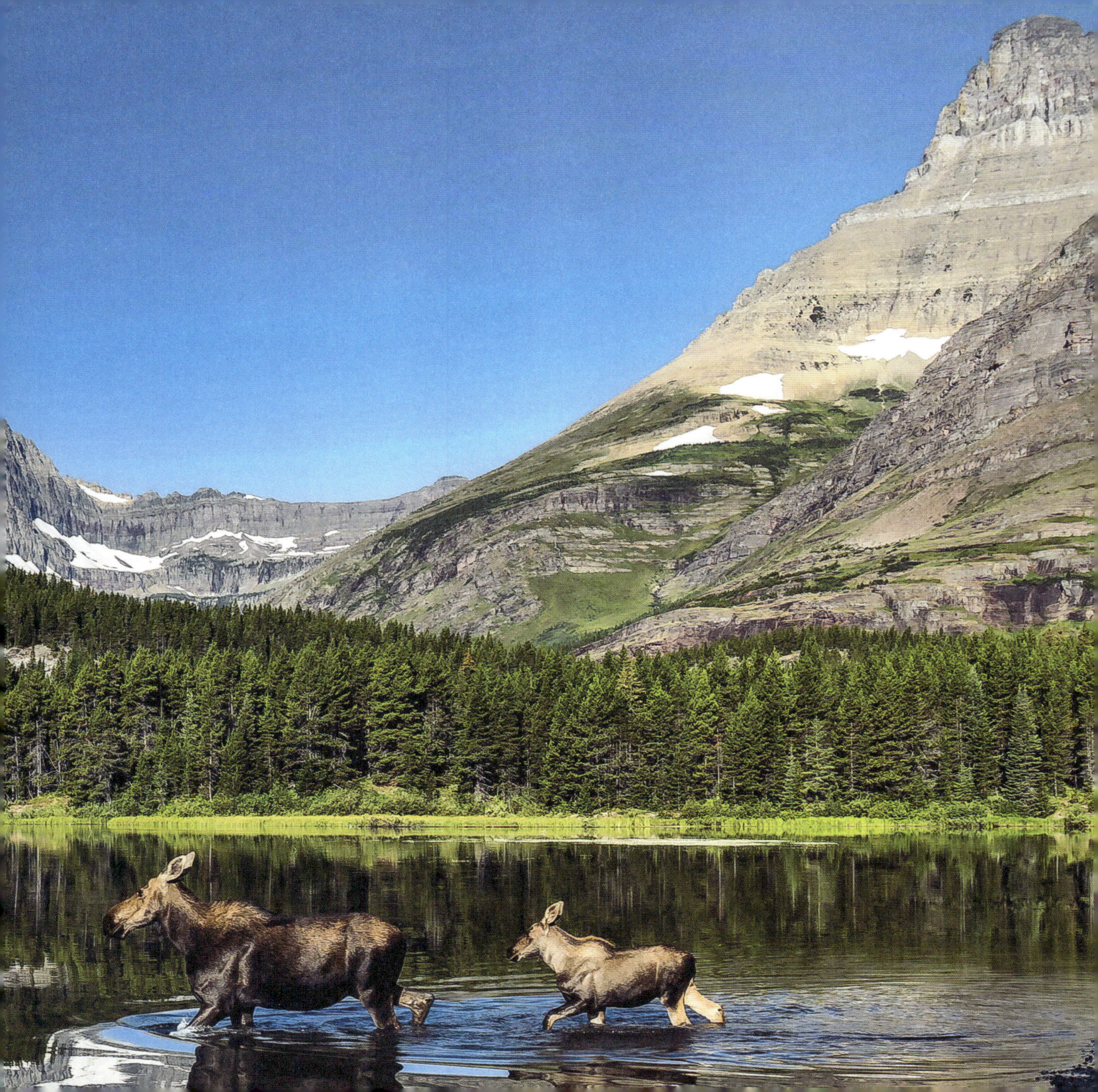

Rocky Mountain
Yellowstone National Park

ESTABLISHED	LOCATION
1872	Northwestern Wyoming
SIZE	**VISITATION NO.**
3,471 square miles	4,501,382

LAND ACKNOWLEDGMENT
Ancestral land of the Shoshone, Kiowa, Crow, Blackfeet, Cayuse, Coeur d'Alene, Nez Perce, Flathead, and Lakota people

FOR MORE INFO, VISIT:
www.nps.gov/yell

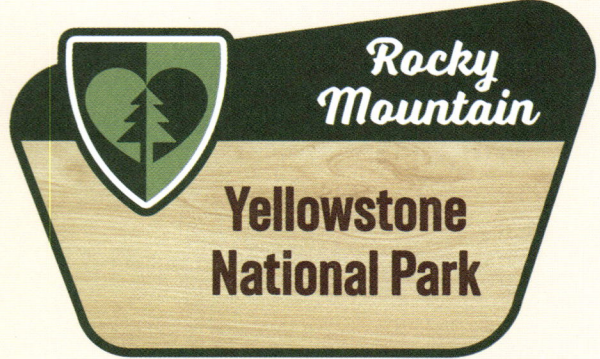

Welcome to America's first national park! Yellowstone National Park is a hotspot, both figuratively and literally. The park boasted over 4 million visitors in 2023, and is also home to approximately 50 percent of the world's hydrothermal features. Yellowstone sits on top of a dormant super-volcano that erupted 70,000 years ago. Besides its famous bison traffic jams, Yellowstone is also known for its captivating gray wolves, which were reintroduced back into the park in 1995 to improve the ecosystem.

Ranger Linda Veress' favorite part of Yellowstone is watching the wildlife roam. "It is a large park at 2.2 million acres and there is something for everyone. Visitors can watch wildlife in an intact ecosystem, explore geothermal areas that contain about half the world's active geysers, and see geologic wonders like the Grand Canyon of the Yellowstone," she explains. "There's something fascinating about watching mud pots bubbling." Ranger Linda also enjoys seeing the happy faces of visitors, especially kids, when they're exploring the park. "It is important for them to know that they are the stewards of this special place," she says, "and it's up to them to preserve and protect it for future generations."

For a park as busy as Yellowstone, Ranger Linda recommends hitting popular spots like Old Faithful and Grand Prismatic Spring either early or late in the day, and to find solitude on a hike even at the busiest times. Her favorite sites? "For me, it's about paying attention and being aware of my surroundings," she says. "For instance, last month I saw the full moon rising with an elk silhouetted against the moonlight and it was really beautiful."

Old Faithful's eruption ranges from 35 to 120 minutes, with an average of 92 minutes between eruptions. It currently erupts about 20 times a day.

Yellowstone National Park
Wyoming

Abyss Pool is one of the deepest hot springs in the park at approximately 53 feet deep.

TRAILBLAZING!

There are four types of thermal features found in Yellowstone: **geysers, hot springs, mud pots,** and **fumaroles**.

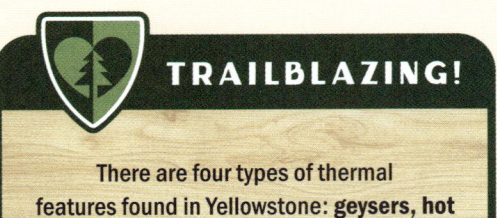

Ranger Valerie Gohlke, who spent nine years at this park before settling in Grand Teton next door, frequently found herself at the West Thumb Geyser Basin, strolling along Black Pool by Yellowstone Lake. "It's probably my favorite hot spring in the entire park and I enjoy sitting there for a very long time," she shares. "It's just mesmerizing, calming, and healing. I love to commune with nature. It's like a magical place."

Her first summer working at Yellowstone, she had the opportunity to be a part of the reintroduction of wolves to the park, after they'd faced extinction for more than 40 years. "To have predators back in the ecosystem, it was amazing," she says. "Yellowstone has so much to offer because it has mountains and rivers and wildlife and meadows and valleys and waterfalls and canyons or the geothermal features."

"Seeing so much wildlife and having bison cross the road in front of our car was a thrill," Chris Zayas, a long-time national park lover, says. "I had always associated Old Faithful with Yellowstone but I had no idea how vast and diverse the park really is. From geysers, mineral deposits, waterfalls, wildlife, and everything in between, it's so much more than I expected."

The travertine terraces are formed from limestone, resembling a cave turned inside out. The color stripes are formed by heat-loving organisms called thermophiles.

Waterfalls abound at Yellowstone.

At Yellowstone, Chris also had a dream came true: to see a moose in the wild. "It was a young bull off the road in a wooded area. A crowd of people had pulled over to take a look and one of them, flirting with danger, decided to flush the moose out by walking into the woods and approaching the moose from behind," she explains. "It was very disturbing to see this kind of recklessness and disrespect for a wild creature. He was lucky, the moose was only mildly irritated and stood up and walked away. We also saw a grizzly bear there and witnessed some visitors, again, approaching too closely. As soon as we saw and identified the bear, we retreated, but it was a thrill to see a grizzly even from a distance."

As a Volunteer-In-Park, I would be remiss if I didn't emphasize the importance of staying a good distance away from wildlife (at least 100 yards from bears and wolves and 25 yards from all other wildlife). Because Yellowstone is so popular, there has been an increase in unsafe behaviors like what Chris witnessed.

Some of my favorite memories from this park are introducing my husband to Yellowstone and both of us checking off our bucket-list item to see gray wolves in the wild. We hired a guide with Wolf Tracker and found a good spot in Lamar Valley to wait for the Junction Butte pack to make their appearance. We saw more than a dozen wolves coming down the hill about a mile from where we were, feasting on a bison carcass while simultaneously charging on a large herd of bison that was grazing nearby.

After several trips to Yellowstone, I've managed to avoid crowds in June and during fall, between mid-September and mid-October. Whatever time of year you choose, take some time to explore the different areas of the park, as each quadrant offers unique landscapes that will make you question if you're still in the same national park!

Yellowstone National Park
Wyoming

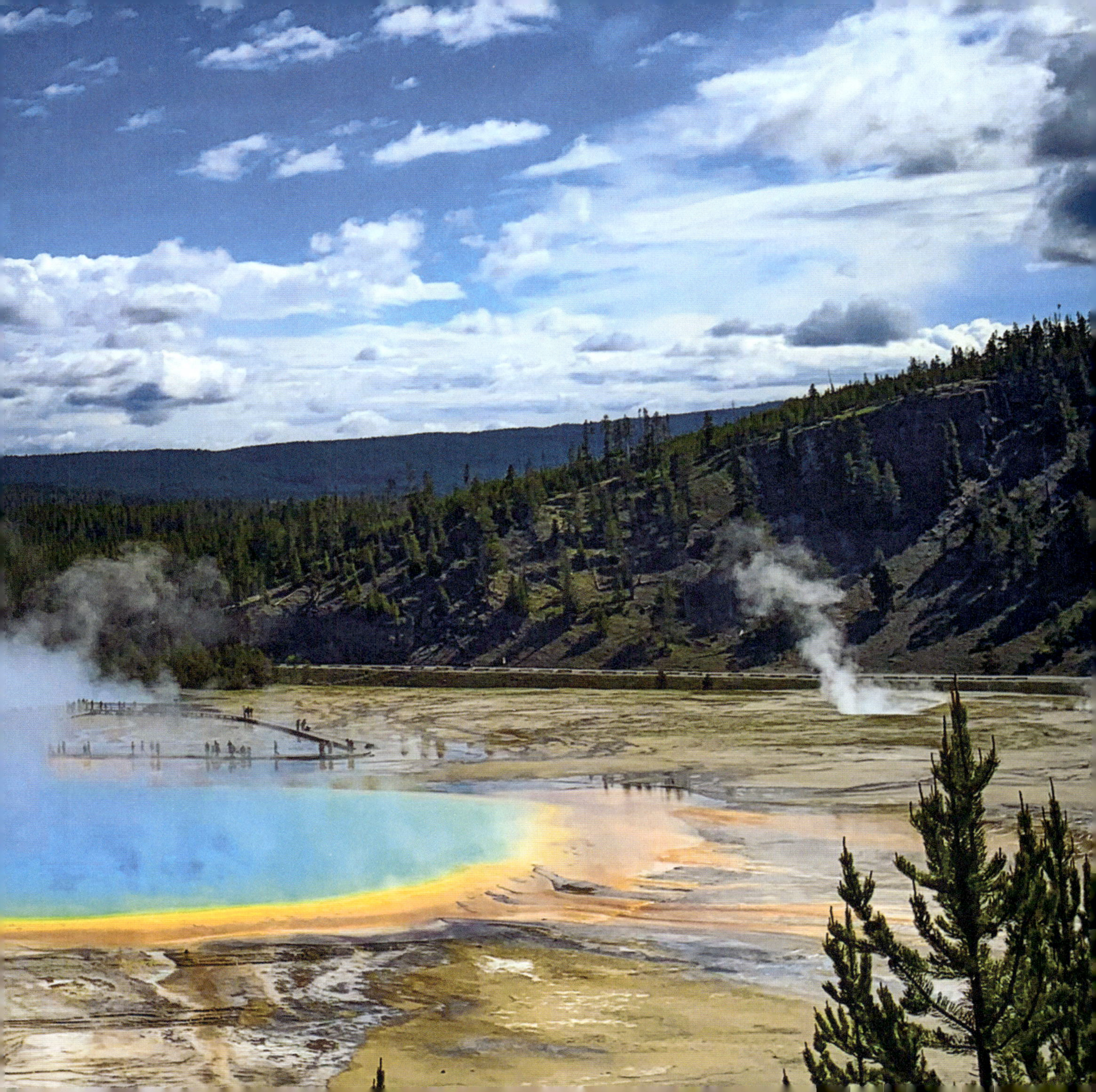

Rocky Mountain
Grand Teton National Park

ESTABLISHED	LOCATION
1929	Northwestern Wyoming

SIZE	VISITATION NO.
485 square miles	3,417,106

LAND ACKNOWLEDGMENT
Ancestral land of the Shoshone, Bannock, Blackfoot, Crow, Flathead, Gros Ventre, and Nez Perce people

FOR MORE INFO, VISIT:
www.nps.gov/grte

Grand Teton National Park provides a breadth of opportunities to enjoy the environment, be it an extreme mountaineering sport or leisurely floating down Snake River during the summer. The park's jagged, snow-capped mountain range and braided rivers shaped the iconic Western landscape.

The Snake River winds through the valley floor, with the Grand Teton range in the background.

As a child, Ranger Valerie Gohlke and her family didn't frequent the national parks, despite living in proximity to a few of them in Florida. She remembers being eight or nine years old, dreaming of working outdoors, living in the woods, and being in the mountains as she listened to musicians like Dan Fogelberg and John Denver. "I applied to be a tour guide in Yellowstone National Park and got hired by the concessionaire," she says. "I flew from Florida to Montana. Having never been west of the Mississippi, I didn't know what I was in for. It ended up being the most spectacular journey to be there that summer. I got impeccable training and really learned the park. I went back to Florida with a 10-year plan that I wanted to work for the National Park Service. The first time I put my ranger flathead on, tears streamed down my face. It was such a dream come true to finally be a park ranger."

Ranger Valerie spent nine years working in Yellowstone before making her way to Grand Teton. Her love for animals made living and working in Grand

TRAILBLAZING!

The Grand Teton Mountain Range is the youngest range in the Rocky Mountains region (formed roughly 775 million years ago), but it's made up by some of the oldest rock found on Earth (from the Precambrian era, dating back 2.7 billion years). Very gneiss!

Teton, known for its wildlife viewing and the beauty of the majestic landscape, perfect. "When I'm standing in front of Jenny Lake and looking at the Teton or Jackson Lake with the Teton in the background, it's just spectacular vistas, breathtaking beauty," she says. "When you're standing in front of a 13,000-plus-feet-tall mountain, you realize how small you are in the scheme of things."

There's so much to see in Grand Teton that Ranger Valerie's best advice is to plan before you visit. Without proper planning, you may not get the most out of your time at the park. She welcomes folks to speak to park rangers at visitor centers for information and to learn about ranger-led programs for the season. "My favorite things to do here are anything that involves the water and the mountains," she adds. "Any of the boat trips, any of the hiking trails along the lakes, I really think that's just some of the most pristine beauty. We also have interesting spots in the park like the Mormon Row Historic District, which is great for both sunrise and sunset."

With over 250 miles of trails to choose from, Grand Teton offers an incredible range of hiking opportunities.

Evan Wexler, a photographer who loves the national parks, was surprised to come across his first (ever) herd of bison crossing the road at Grand Teton, just as a summer storm broke over the mountains. "I felt like I had stepped into a picture in a book; something I had read and heard about for so long was viscerally real," he says. Sarah Olzawski, a fellow national park lover, saw her first

Grand Teton National Park
Wyoming

moose while hiking Cascade Canyon: "My friend joked that I made 'moose face' when I saw the moose, a face of excitement and pure joy!"

Ranger Steve Phan, Chief of Interpretation at the historic Camp Nelson National Monument in Kentucky, thinks about Grand Teton National Park all the time. "I got to go out to Grand Teton for two weeks," he explains. "I shadowed an archaeologist friend there to understand what she does on a daily basis as part of this dynamic cultural resource program at Grand Teton National Park and got to stay in the cabins. Just seeing the space and the mountains, it was miraculous. It really touched my heart how close the staff was, especially the permanent staff that are there year-round. It's not an easy place to live, but the way they support each other is resounding. It is a bucket-list park for me to work at. It is simply my favorite place to be."

A few years ago, I made an intentional "girls' trip" to Grand Teton to meet up with my friends Michelle and Tammy, who flew from Atlanta into Jackson Hole. We spent a three-day weekend exploring Grand Teton, mixing some self-guided hikes on the Taggart Lake and Bradley Lake loop, and walks along Jenny Lake with some tours with the concessionaire.

I booked a tent cabin at Colter Bay Village for our stay (which fit four people). It was a great way to keep the trip affordable and to still "rough it" without having to check any camping equipment onto our flights. We hopped on a narrated Grand Teton bus tour to learn about the geology and overall layout of the park, then went on a scenic river raft trip in late afternoon with supper, and—a first for me—guided horseback ride in the "Old West," departing from Colter Bay Village.

The hike to Delta Lake is usually accessible between June and October, when the trail is clear of snow.

Rocky Mountain

Zion National Park

The most visited of Utah's Mighty Five, Zion almost doesn't need an introduction. Here, you'll find scenic views of massive sandstone monoliths, expansive canyons, and the powerful Virgin River, which carved the spectacular gorge. Zion Canyon sees the most foot traffic from visitors, but with 80 percent of the park designated as wilderness, one can find refuge in the backcountry space or the nearby Kolob Canyon area.

In 2023, Journey Castillo set a record for being the youngest person to visit all the 63 national parks—she was only three! The first national park her parents, Valerie and Eric, took her to was the Grand Canyon, when she was just two weeks old. Valerie Castillo remembers Journey's energy shifting from being at the park: "You can tell in her body language that she was really soaking it up. What we felt like it was doing to our daughter, the energy that she was feeling, this is one of the first few things she's seen with her eyes in the world, so it turned into a passion which quickly became a mission and an obsession." Along the way, Journey visited more than 20 national parks before she turned one. It was at Zion National Park where this little Junior Ranger took her very first step. Eric shares, "For us as parents, that would

Fall colors in Zion National Park are most prominent in October and November.

ESTABLISHED	LOCATION
1909 (redesignated 1919)	Southwestern Utah
SIZE	**VISITATION NO.**
229 square miles	4,623,238

LAND ACKNOWLEDGMENT
Ancestral land of the Pueblo and Southern Paiute people

FOR MORE INFO, VISIT:
www.nps.gov/zion

always be a memory, because that's where she evolved. She was growing up through this journey to the parks and we noticed that."

For Bryan Dinello and his wife, Nazlin Shakir, a hike up to Observation Point was the most harrowing they've ever undertaken, but also one of their favorites because of the difficulties they overcame together. "As novice national park goers, it was already a challenge to tackle one of the more difficult trails in Zion," Bryan says. "After a nerve-wracking exposed climb, a hailstorm greeted us just as we reached the 2,220-feet summit. Then it poured rain as we hugged the cliffs all the way back down. To top it off, we had to wade through a flooded canyon at the base of the mountain. Thankfully the trail was full of seasoned hikers, so we followed their lead and now have a story to tell." Fellow national park lover, Pradeep Chandra, went to Zion for the first time as part of his Utah national parks three-day trip. "It so happened that Angels Landing was my first hike ever. What could top that experience, right? I was so scared to finish the treacherous final section of the trail. I was expecting guard rails and was petrified to learn there were none."

Jonathan Shafer, a park ranger at Zion National Park, shares, "The park doesn't really have a slow season, and this means that we have a lot of great opportunities to connect with visitors who've traveled from across the United States and around the world. Getting to have those conversations is exciting because

Bighorn sheep are most likely seen in the park between the Zion-Mount Carmel Tunnel and the East Entrance.

> **TRAILBLAZING!**
>
> **Kolob Arch** was once thought to be the largest freestanding arch in the world (measured by span), until it was measured and fell three feet short of the Landscape Arch in Arches National Park.

A blind arch is an arch rock still attached to the rock face. The Great Arch in Zion National Park is a prime example of blind arch in the Navajo Sandstone.

it means I get to see the park for the first time through visitors' eyes. Working with Junior Rangers on activities in the park is one of the most fulfilling parts of working in a park, because it's a meaningful opportunity to help (most often young) people find ways to express their interests in order to accomplish the mission of the National Park Service. Helping them understand the ways that they can take action to protect these important places on their first visit and every visit is very meaningful."

Visitors often look to park rangers to help optimize their visits. To Ranger Jonathan, there is no part of the park that isn't a great place to explore. "Whether you end up on a trail that's well known or on an overnight trip in the wilderness, there are great experiences to be had at Zion," he says. "Zion is simply irreplaceable. The National Park Service is dedicated to making sure we conserve special places like Zion so that visitors can enjoy them today and forever."

Zion is exceptionally beautiful in late fall, when the aspen leaves turn yellow against the bright orange of the Navajo sandstone. The temperature can be on the colder side, and you won't find the same level of crowds hiking through the Narrows, a popular trail along the narrowest section of Zion Canyon. The walls along the Narrows are thousands of feet tall and the river, at times, is twenty to thirty feet wide. Although Angels Landing is a bucket list hike for many (it's a one and done for me), I found peace and tranquility along the Watchman trail. It's underrated, and easily accessible from the Watchman Campground near the visitor center. Another personal favorite for me is the Canyon Overlook trail. It's a short walk from the parking lot past the tunnel along Zion-Mount Carmel Highway to a very rewarding view looking down into Pine Creek Canyon and lower Zion Canyon. If the crowds get overwhelming, head over to the Kolob Canyon section of the park, 40 miles north of Zion Canyon. The towering sandstone monoliths there are just as impressive.

Zion National Park
Utah

Zion National Park
Utah

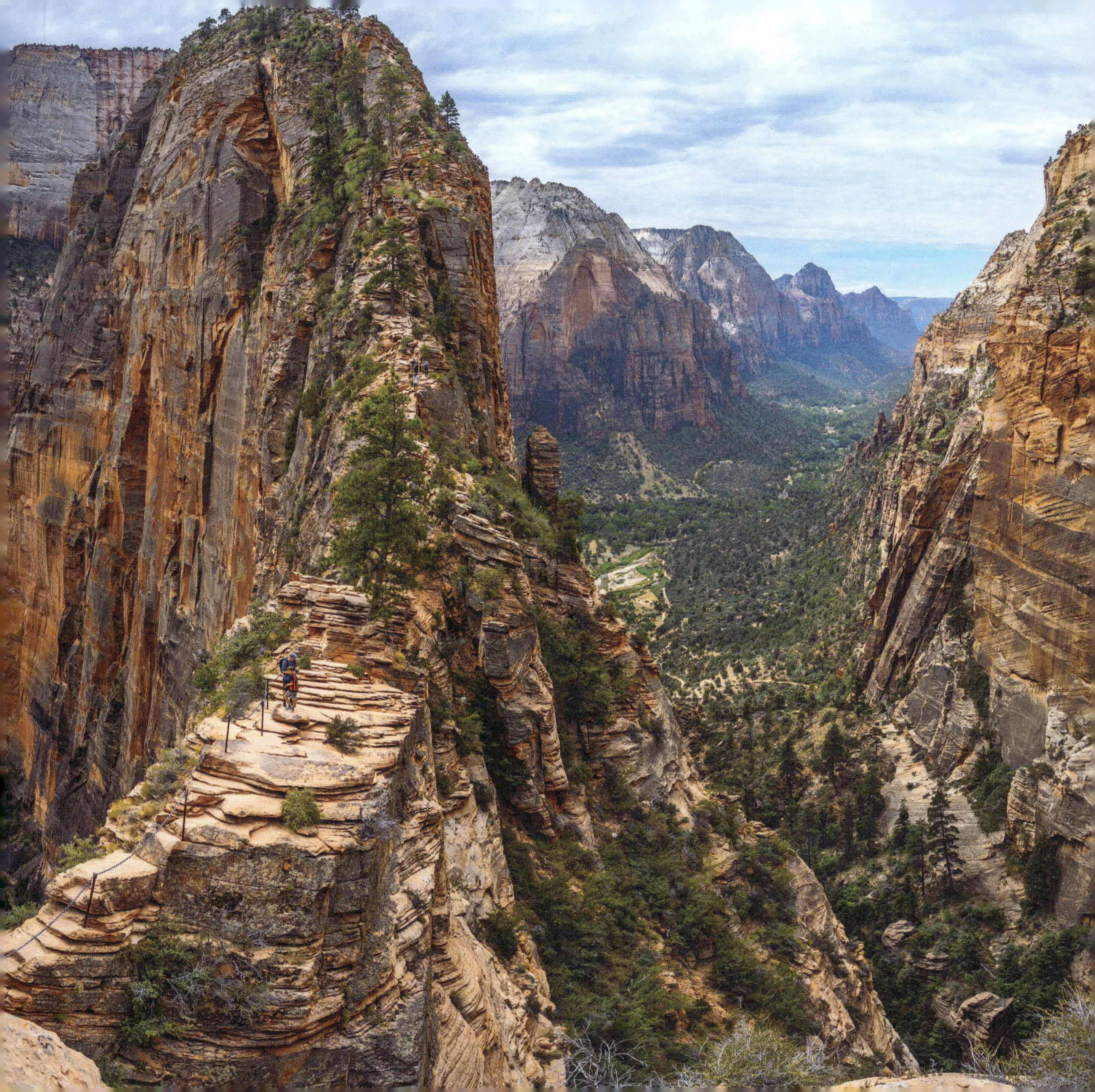

Rocky Mountain

Bryce Canyon National Park

Situated in the unique high desert landscape, the views of an amphitheater filled with rock spires and sandstone hoodoos at Bryce Canyon National Park are otherworldly. A prominent part of the larger Grand Staircase rock formation, exposing an immense sequence of sedimentary rock layers stretching south over a distance of 100 miles, is a sight to behold.

As a kid who lived in the suburbs of Chicago near a cornfield, Ranger Peter Densmore's love relationship with the national parks started when he was leaving Utah to head back to the Midwest after serving several years in the Air Force. On the way, he stopped at Arches National Park so he could truly earn his Utah license plate, which displays the Delicate Arch. A return trip to Utah almost two years later for a friend's wedding brought him to Zion and Bryce Canyon. He recalls his—what the park rangers call—"Bryce moment," when one truly connects with the park. "At that moment in my life, I had no idea that a place like Bryce Canyon existed on the planet, much less within the United States," he says. "I'd never even seen a photo of the place." The next time he returned to Bryce Canyon, he was a park ranger coordinating the 2016 National Park Service Centennial.

One of the park's most iconic hoodoo, Thor's hammer, can be seen while hiking the Navajo Loop Trail.

ESTABLISHED	LOCATION
1923 (redesignated 1928)	Southern Utah
SIZE	**VISITATION NO.**
56 square miles	2,461,269
LAND ACKNOWLEDGMENT	
Ancestral land of the Southern Paiute, Hopi, Zuni, Ute, Pueblo, and Navajo people	
FOR MORE INFO, VISIT:	
www.nps.gov/brca	

Many visitors come to this park to witness the magnificent hoodoos, but Ranger Peter finds beauty in the ponderosa forest on top of the plateau. "It's not the side of Bryce Canyon that people usually think about," he says. "What I really love about Bryce is the contrast between this fragrant open-canopy pine forest, the experience of walking out of that to the edge of the plateau and suddenly having a view that extends over 100 miles across millions years of geology. To move from the intimacy of a forest to suddenly your eye being able to travel these hundreds of miles, I think does something to the brain and the spirit."

If you're planning a visit, Ranger Peter recommends that you consider season, activity, and timing. The park is located 8,000 feet above sea level, so it's often 10°F cooler in the summertime compared to other national parks in Utah, and you can expect piles of snow during winter. But winter also means more solitude, with fewer people and more opportunities to join ranger-led snowshoe hikes. Some wildflowers start blooming in the traditional spring months, but peak wildflowers season will usually arrive in June. Crowds start flocking to Bryce Canyon in March, during spring break, with visitation peaking in June and July before tapering off in October. Come in August if you're looking for nice summer weather with fewer visitors.

Want to see the night sky at the international dark sky park with the longest-running astronomy program at a national park? Plan your trip around the moon phases so you can see the Milky Way or join rangers on a full moon hike. Ranger Peter's favorite moon phase is the night before the full moon. "The moon will come up and it'll look as full as a full moon, but it comes up just before sunset," he explains. "As the sun is setting, the moon is just a little bit up above the horizon. You get the beauty of the moon over the landscape with whatever is

Bryce Canyon is a part of a bigger geologic landscape called the Grand Staircase, a series of colorful sedimentary rock layers that extends 100 miles, from Bryce Canyon to the Grand Canyon.

happening with the sunset. As a photographer, that can create some really beautiful scenes that I love."

Ranger Peter recommends hiking the Rim Trail and making use of the park's free shuttle. Rim Trail connects four of the most popular views in the Bryce Amphitheater area. "My favorite section of the Rim Trail is the mile and a half between Bryce Point and Inspiration Point," he says. "It's usually the quietest section, and it's the highest-elevation section. You can look down on the hoodoos below." The shuttle runs from April to October, so you can hike the Rim Trail one way and take the shuttle back. Alternatively, you can trek the backcountry. Ranger Peter recommends the Riggs Spring Loop Trail down at the Rainbow and Yovimpa points. The trail is 8.5 miles long, so it's doable as a day hike and you're guaranteed to find some solitude.

Bryce Canyon is a popular park and a favorite of many, but it holds a particularly special place in Ranger Peter's heart, and not just because it's where he's worked at for almost a decade. It's the park that gives

Bryce Amphitheater is home to the greatest concentration of hoodoos on Earth.

TRAILBLAZING!

Bryce Canyon has the largest collections of **hoodoos** on Earth. These rock formations were formed by weathering and erosion during the uplift of the Colorado Plateau.

him a sense of renewal after serving in the military. It's the park where he met and married his wife. It feels like home, where he's surrounded by the community that he has built and been a part of since arriving.

"The national park is a place where you can come see superlative beauty," Ranger Peter says. "You can see intact ecosystems, but you've also got the icon of the national park ranger and this long history of interpretation and education. That's the part of the National Park Service that focuses on visitor experience, waiting to greet you and help you understand what you're seeing; then make personal connections to it so that it begins, hopefully, to inspire a lot of things such as conservation. All the things that we want to do for the natural world all start with love. People have to connect with the thing and feel that they care about it personally, and then a lot of those other things often follow. By having a national park experience facilitated by rangers, wayside displays, and all the other sort of methods we use, I imagine that people begin a relationship with the natural world."

The Natural Bridge is technically a natural arch, formed primarily by expansion of ice in cracks within the rock formation.

Rocky Mountain
Capitol Reef National Park

ESTABLISHED	**LOCATION**
1937 (redesignated 1971)	Southern Utah
SIZE	**VISITATION NO.**
378 square miles	1,268,861
LAND ACKNOWLEDGMENT	
Ancestral land of the Ute, Paiute, Navajo, Hopi, Zuni, and Pueblo people	
FOR MORE INFO, VISIT:	
www.nps.gov/care	

Often called the most underrated of Utah's Mighty Five, Capitol Reef undoubtedly offers some of the most stunning geologic outcrops, as evidenced by the famous Waterpocket Fold. Named for eroded depressions in the sandstone, the Waterpocket Fold extends nearly 100 miles, resulting in a dramatic landscape filled with rugged cliffs and canyon while exposing distinctive and colorful rock formations throughout the park.

Hickman Bridge, a 133-foot natural bridge, is one of the highlights of Capitol Reef.

Ranger Shauna Cotrell remembers visiting Zion National Park when she was just three or four years old; she lived in Las Vegas at the time, and her family also often spent time at Lake Mead National Recreation Area and Death Valley National Park. She first considered working for the National Park Service while attending college, but instead chose to work as fisheries bio-technician before joining the Peace Corps and serving two years in the Philippines as a coastal resource management volunteer. She then landed her first seasonal job as park ranger at Everglades National Park and fell in love with the thought of making it a lifetime career.

When it comes to Capitol Reef National Park, Ranger Shauna loves that "there's something for everyone to connect with and experience during a visit. The breathtaking geologic beauty may strike people first but if you look a little closer, there's so much more to discover. There are about 280 million years of Earth's history written in the rocks, and thousands of years of

The Pendleton Barn is part of the Gifford Homestead that lies in the heart of the Fruita Valley.

human history as well. People have been a part of this landscape for at least 10,000 years. Petroglyphs, the Pioneer Register, and the Fruita orchards are all tangible connections to the past. Hundreds of species of plants and animals call the park home, too, many of which are endemic, threatened, or endangered."

If you're only planning on making a quick stop at Capitol Reef as part of your tour of Utah's Mighty Five, Ranger Shauna recommends folks try to spend more time at Capitol Reef, if scheduling allows. "There's so much to explore and having that extra time might allow someone to hike multiple trails, visit the orchards to pick fruit in season, attend ranger talks, and do more without feeling rushed," she says. "Parking areas fill up quickly, so having time and flexibility allows you to visit popular spots when it is less crowded, earlier or later in the day. Around a new moon, the night sky is remarkable, with the Milky Way and thousands of stars from horizon to horizon. If it is near the full moon, consider taking a moonlit walk or hike. If folks have a high clearance vehicle and are comfortable with dirt roads, visiting the more rugged and remote parts of the park opens even more areas to explore." Trail recommendations include Hickman Bridge, Cassidy Arch, and the Cohab Canyon for some "Swiss cheese"-looking rock formations.

The Temple of the Sun monolith is composed of the buff-pink Entrada Sandstone that was deposited some 160 million years ago.

TRAILBLAZING!

This park's name comes from two places: "Capitol," as its **monolithic white domes** of Navajo Sandstone resemble the top of the US Capitol, and "Reef" from the **rocky cliffs** that bar travel, similar to underwater ocean reefs.

Rocky Mountain

Canyonlands National Park

Canyonlands is the largest national park of Utah's Mighty Five, yet it receives the fewest visitors. You're guaranteed to find solitude in Canyonlands, especially compared to nearby neighbor, Arches. The park is geographically divided by the Colorado River and its tributaries into four districts: Island in the Sky, the Needles, the Maze, and the rivers themselves.

Ranger Cadence Cook grew up in Salt Lake City and used to spend Thanksgiving at Zion with her family and friends. She also remembers spending time in Capitol Reef, camping inside the park and the surrounding area at a very early age. Despite the early exposure to public lands, Cadence hasn't always been in love with the outdoors. "I never really thought about being a park ranger until after I graduated college and was trying to figure out what to do," she says. "I took an internship at a national park, which set the wheels in motion. I had a fun time and met some wonderful people. I didn't even think about it as a job opportunity until I finished my internship." Ranger Cadence now works at the Island in the Sky visitor center at Canyonlands.

The area encompassing Canyonlands National Park is expansive, with plenty of recreational opportunities. "I like to take photos. The light in the canyons and the colors in the area are spectacular," Ranger Cadence shares. "I'll drive out one day and it will be just this wonderful sunrise where you'd see things you've never

The Needles District was named for the colorful spires of Cedar Mesa Sandstone that dominate the southeast corner of Canyonlands.

ESTABLISHED	LOCATION
1964	Southeastern Utah
SIZE	**VISITATION NO.**
527 square miles	800,322
LAND ACKNOWLEDGMENT	
Ancestral land of the Ute, Southern Paiute, Pueblo, and Navajo people	
FOR MORE INFO, VISIT:	
www.nps.gov/cany	

Expansive view of Canyonlands National Park, offering a slice of haven for campers and off-roaders alike.

seen before because of the light shining upon them. You always see something because it's a vast open desert, it's beautiful all the time. There's also spectacular hiking in the area. You can fit what people like to do into this park: short hikes or going to the overlooks, backpacking, or even river rafting."

As a park ranger, Cadence enjoys the opportunity to share details with visitors about the park, dark skies, and which trail to hike to see the views. "Learning from and listening to visitors about what they did or saw, as well as how they're having the best day or a great experience at the park, makes the job very rewarding," she says.

Ranger Cadence suggests visitors start in the Island of the Sky District and get their bearings by talking to park rangers at the visitor center. She also reminds you to keep an eye on the weather. "In the summer, it's very hot and in the winter, it's very cold. Then we have our monsoon season, when we get a large amount of rain.

So always making sure that you know what today has in store for you makes a huge difference."

Ranger Cadence's favorite spots in the park are the classic Mesa Arch and Grandview Point, both of which offer spectacular views. "There's a reason that they're the most popular spots," she says. "Personally, I also like Green River Overlook. It has great light for sunset."

TRAILBLAZING!

Canyonlands contains some of the last remote areas left in the contiguous US. The park's **Maze District** is the least accessible, and visitors are expected to be self-sufficient, properly equipped, and prepared to self-rescue.

Rocky Mountain

Arches National Park

ESTABLISHED 1929 (redesignated 1971)	**LOCATION** Southeastern Utah
SIZE 119 square miles	**VISITATION NO.** 1,482,045
LAND ACKNOWLEDGMENT Ancestral land of the Southern Ute, Southern Paiute, Hopi, Pueblo, and Navajo people	
FOR MORE INFO, VISIT: www.nps.gov/arch	

Home of the iconic Delicate Arch, which is widely displayed on one of Utah's license plates, Arches National Park has the densest concentration of natural stone arches in the world. To date, the park has documented well over 2,000 arches, along with other interesting geologic formations such as pinnacles, fins, and balanced rocks.

The first national park that Ranger Karen Garthwait visited as a child was also the first one that she worked at. Her career with the National Park Service started at Lassen Volcanic National Park, when she responded to an ad seeking volunteers with museum and library experience. She later came to consider the entire experience a "rebirth." Since then, Ranger Karen has worked at several other parks, though she's now been at Arches for almost two decades.

The park offers a variety of experiences, whether you're short on time or are eager to go miles into the backcountry. "The Park Avenue scenic road takes you right through the center of the park and there's a lot that you could see without leaving your car," Ranger Karen explains. "Alternatively, over 90 percent of the park is qualified as proposed wilderness. There are no trails or roads in those parts of the park, but if you know how to explore safely and without causing any damage by staying on bare rock or existing drainages where water flows where the living soil cover called biological soil crust (biocrust) isn't

Sandstone wall formations seen from the La Sal Mountains Viewpoint in the park.

The Tower of Babel is a popular rock-climbing spot at Arches.

TRAILBLAZING!

Biocrust is made up of oxygen-generating living organisms like mosses, green algae, fungi, and cynobacteria, and acts as a protective layer, holding the desert floor together so the materials underneath do not wash away when it rains.

going to form there, you can do so. That's why I feel like Arches really has something for everyone: the one-hour visitor, the half-day visitor, a family, or someone who just wants to be alone in the desert with their thoughts."

Ranger Karen stresses the importance of getting the most updated park information via the park's website and social media, instead of relying on outdated guidebooks. As for park activities, she says, "A lot of people who come to Arches already have some must-haves in mind, like the Delicate Arch. My recommendation is wherever you go, take a couple of minutes to just sit down and enjoy being where you are. Let the stillness, the age of these rocks, sit with you. Know that quiet of the desert. When people have rushed through their travels, it's easy to forget to do that. And you're missing out on something that these parks can offer you, which is just that refuge for the soul. I do love these places and I love inspiring other people to discover that they love them too."

One of the most popular places to visit at Arches is the Windows section, where you can spot at least half a dozen major arches just by turning in a circle. There are also a few short hiking trails that will get you underneath some arches. "I always recommend people at least drive

The iconic view of Delicate Arch, as seen on many Utah license plates.

Arches National Park
Utah

through there," Ranger Karen says. The 1-mile (round trip) trail will lead you to Turret Arch, North Window, South Window, and the Double Arch. Other named prominent rock formation features in this area include Garden of Eden, Elephant Butte, and Parade of Elephants.

For national park lover Tavia Carlson, one of her favorite memories is taking her kids on an early-morning hike to see Delicate Arch. "The kids and I woke up a couple hours before dawn and hiked in the pitch black to reach Delicate Arch for sunrise. It was something I had wanted to do for so long and watching my two little kids hike with headlamps and then sit to watch the incredible sunrise was amazing. A stranger and I traded taking photos and they are some of my most treasured park images."

My first experience in Arches National Park was during a geology field trip when I was in graduate school. I vividly remember falling in love with red rocks and sandstone for the very first time, as my group hiked towards Delicate Arch and witnessed the sunset. We looked at rocks for days, flip-flopping between Arches and Canyonlands in search of the horst and graben (valley and range) geologic formations resulting from the tectonic process. It took me a decade to return to this park. On my last visit to Arches, I stopped by Balanced Rock, hiked the short trail to the Double Arch and Windows area, and did the same Delicate Arch hike for sunset, now with a better appreciation and understanding of the landscape and the need to protect such natural gems. To me, Arches National Park is a geologic wonderland, and a place that everyone should experience at least once in their lifetime.

The Double Arch towering feature is the tallest arch in the park.

Rocky Mountain

Mesa Verde National Park

Historical, heritage, and homey, Mesa Verde National Park protects a sacred place where the Ancestral Pueblo people lived and thrived on the mesas and in the cliffs for over 700 years. Today, the park provides visitors a spectacular window into the rich cultural heritage of 26 Indigenous tribes.

For Ranger Shannon Roberts, Mesa Verde is a place that is as much about the future as it is about the past. He grew up in West Virginia and often drove across the New River Bridge to visit family within the state. His

ESTABLISHED	LOCATION
1906	Southwest Colorado
SIZE	VISITATION NO.
81 square miles	505,194
LAND ACKNOWLEDGMENT	
Ancestral land of the Pueblo people	
FOR MORE INFO, VISIT:	
www.nps.gov/meve	

The Cliff Palace is the largest known cliff dwelling in North America. A 45-minute, ranger-led tour is available via ticketed reservation.

career with the National Park Service didn't start until when he was almost 40, after he went on a 10,000-mile road trip across the country for over two months and spent time camping at many national parks. "I was hooked and went to college, where I interned with parks during the summer," he says, "and I have worked in parks since I graduated. For me, it's the 'education, and inspiration of this and future generations' part of the National Park Service's mission that drew me to the agency. I am an educator and believe that it is very important work to prepare our next generation to be the stewards and caretakers of our most special and sacred places."

As the Education Program Coordinator at Mesa Verde National Park, Ranger Shannon enjoys connecting visitors to the ongoing story of perseverance and resilience of the Ancestral Puebloan. The most fun part of the job is "goofing off with kids and having so much fun" while teaching them the history of the place and its people. "Mesa Verde National Park is a story of a people's deep and continued connection with a landscape," he explains. "There are 26 tribes and Pueblos of Indigenous people that have connections to this place, and it is very powerful."

Before visiting, Ranger Shannon says, "a little more planning is necessary to make sure you'll be able to do all the things you'd like for your trip, so make sure to use the website and plan, plan, plan. Be sure to book those ranger tours in advance! I love the Far View Sites at Mesa Verde. It is an ancient village site that is part of a much larger community that lived on top of the mesa. It's a great place for an easy hike and to learn about where most of the population of Mesa Verde lived."

I suggest opting for an overnight stay at the Far View Lodge inside the park. It provides some of the best views in the Four Corners region (where the corners of Utah, Arizona, Colorado, and New Mexico meet). You'll also have the opportunity to dine at Spruce Tree Terrace Café and feast on Southwest Navajo tacos—Native American fry bread piled high with a hearty amount of toppings—with stellar views from the patio.

For more than 700 years, the Ancestral Pueblo people built thriving communities on the mesas and in the cliffs of Mesa Verde.

TRAILBLAZING!

The Cliff Palace is the largest and most famous cliff dwelling in the park, with over 150 individual rooms and more than 20 kivas (space for religious rituals). It's believed that this palace held about 100 people, implying its significance as a social, administrative, and ceremonial spot.

Rocky Mountain

Black Canyon of the Gunnison National Park

ESTABLISHED	**LOCATION**
1933 (redesignated 1999)	Western Colorado
SIZE	**VISITATION NO.**
47 square miles	357,069
LAND ACKNOWLEDGMENT	
Ancestral land of the Ute people	
FOR MORE INFO, VISIT:	
www.nps.gov/blca	

The landscape of Black Canyon of the Gunnison is two million years in the making, including a deep canyon, steep cliffs, and some of the craggiest spires you'd seen in North America. At its narrowest point, the canyon is just 40 feet wide at river level.

As a park lover who has visited more than 260 National Park Service units, Ranger Lori Rome's journey through America's Best Idea started when she was young. "My parents were teachers, and we would travel to national parks each summer in our motorhome," she says. "I have memories of being a very young child visiting Yellowstone, Yosemite, and Grand Canyon." She then pursued her undergraduate degree in geography and geology and was fascinated after taking a Geology of National Parks class. Some of Ranger Lori's favorite national parks are Grand Canyon, Mount Rainier, and Olympic, for their awesome ecology, geology, and hiking trails.

Ranger Lori loves Black Canyon of the Gunnison for its landscapes and night skies. The canyon is spectacular both day and night. "An average visit to Black Canyon of the Gunnison lasts around half a day.

Gunnison River, which runs through the park, is one of the largest tributaries of the Colorado River.

> ## TRAILBLAZING!
>
> The **Gunnison River** drops an average of 43 feet per mile over the length of Black Canyon of the Gunnison, which is almost six times of the Colorado River in the Grand Canyon.

I encourage visitors to stop at the park's co-managed site, Curecanti National Recreation Area," she says. "Curecanti is part of the same geology as Black Canyon, and the Gunnison River passes through both park units. At Curecanti, there are hikes that lead folks into the Black Canyon, like the Curecanti Creek Trail, which is amazing. Curecanti is less visited, so not as busy and lets folks get into the canyon and to the river."

There are several walking paths on the South Rim of Black Canyon, where you can catch great views. Painted Wall, the tallest cliff in Colorado, can be viewed from the Painted Wall View Overlook, the closest view available from the rim. For a picture-perfect view of the entirety of Painted Wall, hike along the Cedar Point Nature Trail, where you'll get to see it from the river to the rim. The North Rim of the canyon doesn't receive as many visitors, so for sunrise lovers or solitude seekers, witnessing the stunning pink and orange light shining across the Painted Wall at Chasm View can be a phenomenal core memory experience.

The Black Canyon is named as such due to its steepness, which makes it difficult for sunlight to penetrate into its depths, causing the rocky walls to appear black.

Rocky Mountain National Park

Every fall, elk descend from the high country to the meadow for their annual breeding season.

Spanning the Continental Divide, Rocky Mountain is known for its mountains, aspen forest, alpine tundra, and lakes. It is a classic national park, filled with beautiful landscapes and a plethora of big mammals like elk, moose, bears, bighorn sheep, mule deer, and mountain lions.

Ranger Jamie Richards' first national park was Rocky Mountain National Park, so working here now is a full-circle moment. "I remember being about three years old and going hiking with my dad," she shares. "For my family, going on vacation meant visiting national parks, museums, or other public lands. I developed a love for history and the outdoors through these experiences. By the age of 17, I had visited many national park sites across the US through Girl Scouts trips and traveling with my family."

Her interest in becoming a park ranger was first piqued when she was twelve, while visiting Black Canyon of the Gunnison. "We were on a boat tour of the canyon and I remember seeing the park ranger on the boat and thinking, 'She was so cool. Being a park ranger would be a fun job. I'd like to do that one day,'" she recalls. "As a senior in college, when I was considering what job or internship to pursue after graduation, I had the opportunity to apply for an internship with the National Park Service through the Student Conservation Association." That first internship later opened the door to her career with the National Park Service.

ESTABLISHED	LOCATION
1915	Northern Colorado

SIZE	VISITATION NO.
415 square miles	4,115,837

LAND ACKNOWLEDGMENT
Ancestral land of the Ute and Arapaho people

FOR MORE INFO, VISIT:
www.nps.gov/romo

Rocky Mountain National Park
Colorado

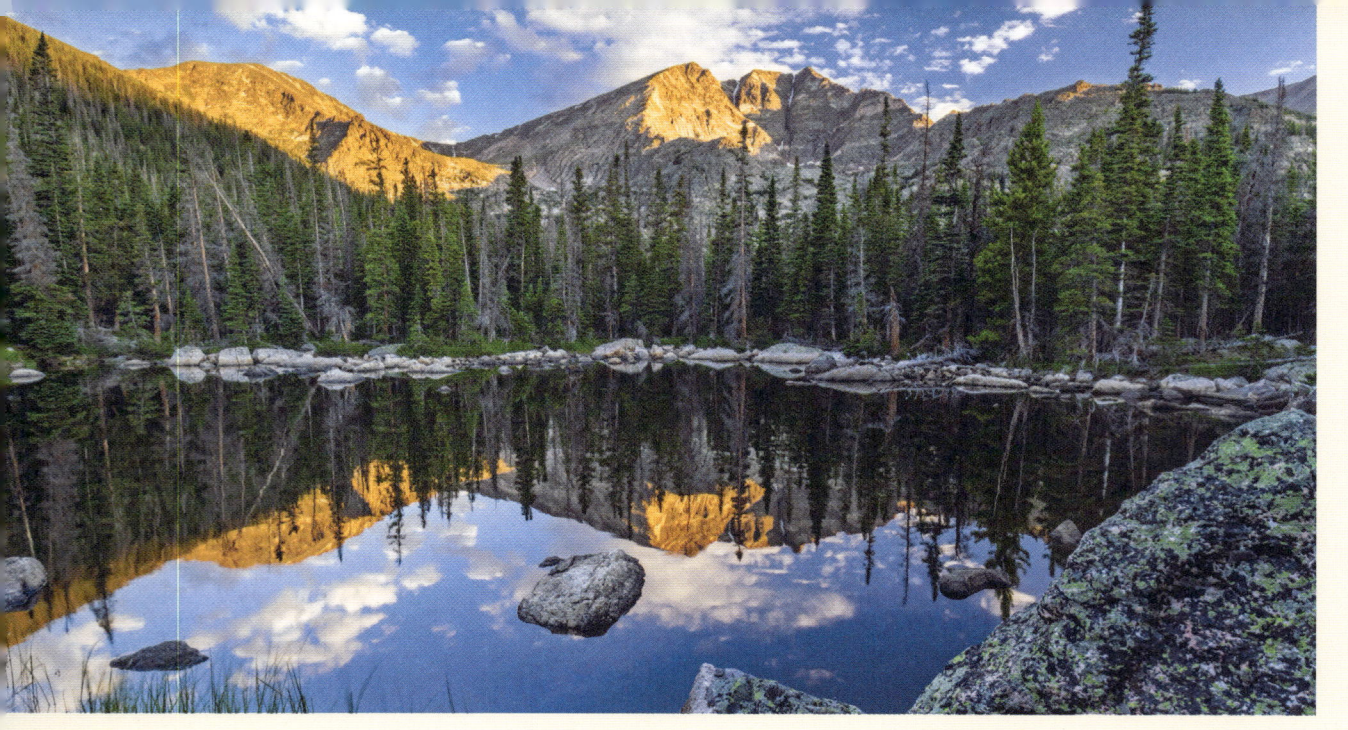

A beautiful reflection of the Rockies at Chipmunk Lake.

For visitors planning a visit to the Rockies, Ranger Jamie recommends coming in the spring and fall. "In March and April, temperatures are beginning to warm up and there is still snow on many trails," she says. "For those interested in history, visit the west side of Rocky Mountain and explore the Holzwarth Historic Site. The grounds are open year-round, 24 hours a day. Enjoy a walk on a trail along the banks of the Colorado River and take in the views of the Never Summer Mountains in the distance. This area also offers excellent fishing and wildlife viewing opportunities."

Ranger Jamie's favorite aspect of the park is how dramatically the landscape varies throughout the year. "It's an incredible wilderness park with exceptional wildlife viewing opportunities available year-round," she says. "Winter offers quiet opportunities for solitude, when the landscape is covered in a blanket of fresh snow. For those who enjoy snowshoeing, this is a great place to explore December through mid-May. As winter

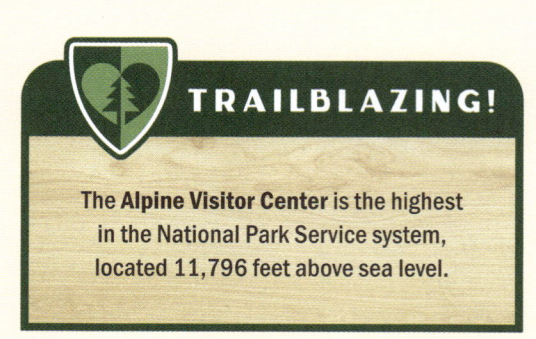

TRAILBLAZING!

The **Alpine Visitor Center** is the highest in the National Park Service system, located 11,796 feet above sea level.

and spring snow melts and summer returns, alpine lakes sparkle with mountain peaks towering overhead. Meadows and the alpine tundra are covered with an array of wildflowers. Wildlife like bighorn sheep, elk, magpies, marmots, and pika are common."

Rocky Mountain also holds special memories for many of the national park lovers in this book, myself included. This was the first national park I visited, when I was just a sophomore in college and living in Golden, Colorado. I had a group of Malaysian friends visiting from Wisconsin, and the park came up as one of the popular places to visit nearby. I did not know what to expect, but I still have a vivid memory of seeing a herd of elk for the first time as we were exiting the park and having no idea what those big animals were.

Rocky Mountain was also the first national park for Matt and Karen Smith, the authors of Dear Bob and Sue. The couple traveled to all 59 (at the time) big parks after becoming empty-nesters. Karen shares, "We quit our jobs and set off, thinking it would take us a year to see them all. It ended up taking us two years, but it was the most rewarding and life-changing thing we've ever done. Matt and I never visited any national parks while growing up in Kansas, and it wasn't until we were married with young children of our own that we discovered Rocky Mountain National Park on a visit to Estes Park, Colorado. Our family had so much fun exploring the park, and driving up Trail Ridge Road to the Alpine Visitor Center, the highest visitor center in the National Park Service system. We will always remember our children's faces as they played joyfully in the snow up there (in July!), and when they saw a herd of elk for the very first time. This park became our annual summer vacation trip."

Corey Ford, whose first park was also Rocky Mountain, remembers the experience as if it was just yesterday. "I remember feeling small up against that landscape," he recalls. "I remember having absolutely no cell reception and not caring that I was disconnected. I remember trying to drive up Trail Ridge Road and feeling the effects of altitude. I remember how all these thoughts piqued my interest in exploring the park further with more preparation."

Bryan Dinello recalls beating the rush to Bear Lake with his wife, Nazlin, and having the "magically serene place" to themselves. "It was so quiet and peaceful with just us and the chipmunks," he shares. "Later, on a stroll towards Nymph Lake, we encountered a family of elk and watched as they crossed our path and found their breakfast just feet away. It was beautiful to feel connected to their world even for a few minutes. At Rocky Mountain National Park driving is an experience on its own. As you cruise up Trail Ridge Road—aka 'the Highway to the Sky'—it's astounding to see the terrain shift from open meadows to dense forest and eventually to the alpine tundra above the treeline. Everything changes and it feels like you're traveling between completely different worlds, all on the same road. Since it's the highest paved road in the US, be sure to pull over and take breaks if you get light-headed like me!"

Rocky Mountain National Park
Colorado

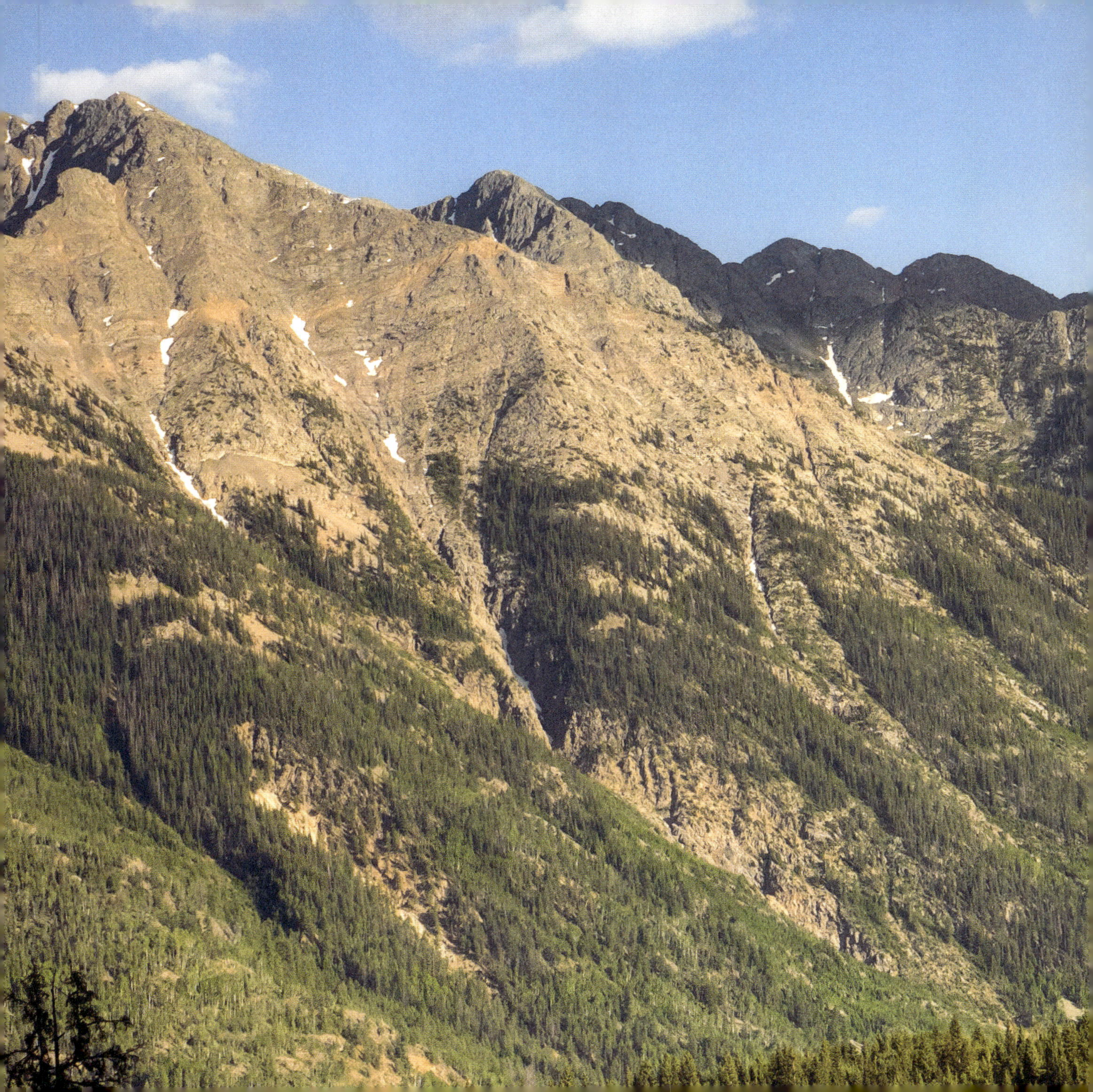

Rocky Mountain

Great Sand Dunes National Park

Great Sand Dunes National Park was designated to protect a massive area filled—as the name suggests—with sand dunes. And not just your typical sand dunes: this park is home to the tallest dunes in North America. It also encompasses diverse landscapes of grasslands, wetlands, alpine lakes, tundra, and forests.

Ranger Zack Brown grew up in the suburbs of Denver, a quick drive away from Rocky Mountain National Park, the first national park he ever visited. I met Ranger Zack when he was a seasonal ranger at Acadia, but today, he is a permanent park ranger at Great Sand Dunes.

Not all park rangers have a solid background in environmental science or history. In fact, Ranger Zack's family was predominantly focused on information technology and computer-based professions. He started down a similar path in high school before he realized he wanted to be outside, educating people about nature. He pivoted into forestry and then, after a few years of being a zip-line guide, he landed his very first seasonal job as ranger at Glacier National Park.

Ranger Zack enjoys the wide variation of resources that Great Sand Dunes helps to manage and protect. "I enjoy helping visitors in finding their passion for the outdoors or in the parks themselves," he says, though, "the Junior Ranger program is a close second." Ranger Zack loves spending time on the mountainside trails. With his background in forestry, he prefers to be with the tall trees rather than the sandy beach. "We are more than just a park," he says. "We also have the preserve designation and most of that land is in the mountains and alpine."

As many other rangers have said, Ranger Zack reminds Great Sand Dunes visitors to plan ahead and expect to wait at the entrance during peak season. "With a single-road access, wait times can be at least an hour just to enter," he warns, but, "We're in the works of a transportation and transit plan to understand, better accommodate, and provide a better experience for the growing number of visitors who are interested in the

ESTABLISHED	LOCATION
1932 (redesignated 2007)	Southern Colorado
SIZE	VISITATION NO.
167 square miles	512,219
LAND ACKNOWLEDGMENT	
Ancestral land of the Ute, Cheyenne, Apache, Navajo and Pueblo people	
FOR MORE INFO, VISIT:	
www.nps.gov/grsa	

The tallest sand dunes in North America, measuring up to 750 feet tall, are found in this park.

park." And if you plan to slide down the dunes, know that there are no rentals within the park, so rent your sleds in advance.

Chris Zayas and her family love this park. "The day we arrived, it was very windy. We began hiking into the sand dunes and it felt like my feet were in quicksand while the wind pelted my arms and legs with grains of sand that stung like bees," she remembers. "My family seemed to have no trouble navigating the dunes, so I told them to go ahead and I followed more slowly behind. I took many photos of the dunes with their soft, rolling folds and the shadows they created."

TRAILBLAZING!

The sand at the park can move—and sing! Sand moves via the **saltation mechanism**, in which particles of sand are picked up by the wind and land back on the surface, and a **humming sound** is made when air pushes through tumbling sand grains during an avalanche when a storm rolls in.

Rocky Mountain

Theodore Roosevelt National Park

ESTABLISHED	LOCATION
1947 (redesignated 1978)	Western North Dakota
SIZE	VISITATION NO.
110 square miles	746,862
LAND ACKNOWLEDGMENT	
Ancestral land of the Mandan, Hidatsa, and Arikara people	
FOR MORE INFO, VISIT:	
www.nps.gov/thro	

Badlands and bison sprawl across the rugged landscape of Theodore Roosevelt National Park, a sight to behold in the sweeping plains that are home to a diverse wildlife population. President Theodore Roosevelt's time spent hunting bison in this Dakota Territory left a significant impression on him that forever altered the course of conservation and preservation in the United States.

Bison were first introduced to the park in 1956, when 29 bison were brought in from Fort Niobrara National Wildlife Refuge in Nebraska.

Andrew Fisher, too, spent some time in this region while he was living in North Dakota. "My experience with national parks started in 2013 with a great group of friends and has grown in the years since," he says. "I've visited 40 national parks so far, some multiple times. Theodore Roosevelt National Park has an abundance of wildlife like no other. Bison, prairie dogs, wild horse, elk, pronghorn, longhorn cattle, and more than 180 types of birds are often visible from the road, making this a great 'drive-through' park."

Geographically, the park consists of three individual units: the North, the South, and Elkhorn Ranch. Andrew shares, "North Unit offers a much more drastic change in elevation, with the beautiful badlands stretching as far as the eye can see. It's my go-to for backpacking trips because of the stunning views and challenging trails." The South Unit has similar landscapes to the

Little Missouri River meanders through the park, supporting a wide variety of plants and animals.

North, but sees more visitors due to its proximity to the town of Medora.

Ranger Maureen McGee-Ballinger, the Deputy Superintendent at Theodore Roosevelt National Park, says her favorite part of the park is the Elkhorn Ranch Unit. "It's where Theodore Roosevelt built his ranch, providing him a place of healing and solace after the deaths of his wife and his mother. The ranch structure no longer exists except for a few flagstones, and it takes some extra time and effort to get to this isolated location. However, a visit to the ranch site can provide a glimpse into what Roosevelt experienced on the Little Missouri River, among the cottonwood trees, and colorful buttes," she explains. "Another amazing and almost unknown spot is the Petrified Forest area in the South Unit of the park. Accessing the location requires either a long backcountry hike or driving outside the South Unit." This park is home to the third-highest concentration of petrified wood in the United States.

Mick Dees, a photographer, hiker, and national park enthusiast, was surprised on his trip to Theodore Roosevelt to learn that Yellowstone isn't the only place that experiences bison traffic jams. "I hiked the Wind Canyon Trail in the South Unit for sunset, and came back to my Jeep to find a herd of bison had surrounded it, leaving me in the awkward position of having to just sit and wait it out. Not sure if you've ever seen a bison graze, but it's not a fast process! Eventually, I set off my Jeep alarm, which caused them to move enough that I could pass by and leave."

TRAILBLAZING!

The **black-tailed prairie dog** can be found in this park by the thousands. They live in prairie dog towns, where a series of burrows are connected underground via tunnels. Roosevelt himself called them "the most noisy and inquisitive animals imaginable." He was spot on.

Rocky Mountain
Wind Cave National Park

Slow-moving water dissolves limestone at the edges, exposing crystal fins called boxwork.

A number of caves are protected under the National Park Service system, but only one has the world's largest concentration of rare boxwork formations: thin blades of calcite projecting from cave walls and ceilings at various angles, forming "boxes" on cave surfaces. Wind Cave National Park is the first cave to be designated as a national park, and this place holds a significant history for the Lakota people. The Emergence Story passed orally from one generation to another says that near the natural entrance of Wind Cave is a portal between the spirit lodge underground and the spirit world on the surface of the Earth.

Ranger Lydia Jones works as a seasonal ranger at Wind Cave National Park. Born to a traveling nurse, Lydia grew up traveling, before settling down right outside Big Bend National Park when she was eight. "I never actually once considered being a park ranger," she admits. "I was dead set on being a paleontologist. Then I got older and thought that wasn't a realistic career path, so I majored in biology in college. I ended up going back to fossils and became an educator at a paleontology exhibit at a big science museum in Texas. Then 2020 happened and I got laid off. I heard of this program called Scientists in Parks that has internships in national parks. It was a light-bulb moment for me."

For Ranger Lydia, getting to work in a cave is the coolest thing about being a park ranger at Wind Cave. "I love that Wind Cave is really like two parks in one. You

ESTABLISHED	LOCATION
1903	Southwestern South Dakota
SIZE	VISITATION NO.
44 square miles	592,459
LAND ACKNOWLEDGMENT	
Ancestral land of the Lakota and Cheyenne people	
FOR MORE INFO, VISIT:	
www.nps.gov/wica	

Prairies and grasslands of Wind Cave National Park.

have this amazing cave system underground and then up top, you have the beautiful prairie, the ponderosa pine forest ecosystem, and all these hiking trails," she explains. "Then you've got wildlife viewing. We have a bison herd here, so it's the best of both worlds as far as a park goes." She loves sharing her love for national parks with visitors and making connections with people who travel from all over the world, teaching them about what the park is protecting. "I think that's so important for cultivating that sense of stewardship in our society and in the next generation," she says.

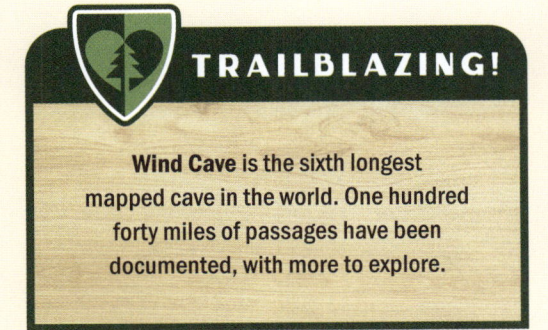

TRAILBLAZING!

Wind Cave is the sixth longest mapped cave in the world. One hundred forty miles of passages have been documented, with more to explore.

You need to be on a ticketed, ranger-led tour to enter the cave. When choosing a tour, consider your availability, ability to navigate the number of stairs, the distance, and the duration of each tour, which can be found on the park's website. Ranger Lydia's favorite is the Fairgrounds Tour, where you explore the middle level of the cave to see the boxwork formation, then head to the upper level for popcorn and frostwork formations. Bobby Beaulieu and his national-park-loving family opted for the Natural Entrance Tour. "We learned a lot about all the unique features of caves, such as cave bacon (or draperies), and fell in love with caves."

Book your tickets ahead of time to secure the preferred cave tour during the visit.

Badlands National Park

Rocky Mountain

ESTABLISHED	LOCATION
1939 (redesignated 1978)	Southwestern South Dakota

SIZE	VISITATION NO.
379 square miles	1,046,400

LAND ACKNOWLEDGMENT
Ancestral land of the Lakota people

FOR MORE INFO, VISIT:
www.nps.gov/badl

Contrary to its name, there's nothing bad about the land at Badlands National Park, aside from it being unsuitable for farming. The scenery is dramatic, spanning layers of rock formations that often change color after rain or snow, or whenever the sun hits the steep canyons and the towering spires. Buried amongst these geologic deposits is one of the world's richest fossil beds, where ancient rhinos and horses once roamed.

Ranger Aaron Kaye was born to a park ranger dad and grew up in a number of national parks through the years. "My first national park I can relate to is Hawai'i Volcanoes National Park," he shares. "My dad was the Chief of Interpretation park ranger there during the 1976 Kilauea caldera eruptions. I remember the earthquake that preceded that because it broke things in the house. My dad jumped into his uniform, grabbed his camera gear, and headed out to the outer edge of the crater to take photos of the eruption. At a certain point he called up my mom to bring us kids to the crater, since there was a chance we'd never see anything like that again." He

These striking geologic deposits contain one of the world's richest fossil beds.

grew up surrounded by the green and gray uniform, but his dad actually asked him to be a lawyer or a doctor instead.

Despite the request, Ranger Aaron became a seasonal ranger at Mesa Verde before securing a permanent position at the Grand Canyon. He has now been at Badlands for more than 25 years. His favorite part about Badlands is his short but beautiful commute to work: "I live approximately a three-minute walk from the visitor center. My daily commute comes with the backdrop of the badlands." He also enjoys the fishing. "You never would think that there was a spectacular fishing opportunity here," he says. "I would call it my church. More than just an active sport, it's a spiritual experience. A way to enjoy nature that attracted me here at the Badlands." He also enjoys the unique experience of bison roundup, part of the park's resource management plan. "The carrying capacity of the environment that the bison are in over on the western side of the park can only hold a limited number of animals due to lack of water and grass. At the moment, we try to keep the population to around 800 to 1,000 bison, and we give a percentage of them to the Indigenous population in the area."

Ranger Aaron loves sharing resources with visitors, be it their first time to the park or their hundredth.

Prickly pear cactus with towering badland spires in the background.

"Badlands is one of those places that really strikes people when they come here," he says. "A lot of people are just super excited and kind of stunned at what they see, and obviously the beauty of the area as the park changes with the seasons. I really enjoy sharing the night sky with visitors during our night sky program at the park. This past year has been pretty spectacular. We're far enough north that when the Kp Index [level of geomagnetic activity] is about five, you can start seeing the aurora borealis at the Door and Window Trailhead parking lots."

Badlands National Park
South Dakota

Badlands is an open park where you can hike off-trail (except in certain designated areas), but be mindful of your capabilities and personal safety.

> ### TRAILBLAZING!
> Badlands has the nation's largest expanses of **mixed-grass prairie ecosystem**, with grasses ranging from ankle height to waist height. The semi-arid climate, where rainfall is low and unpredictable, makes an ideal environment for the grass to grow.

The weather at the park can change drastically, so it's wise to be prepared. "This is an open park, so you don't have to stay on trails. As such, you are limited by your own abilities, so know your limits and honor them," Ranger Aaron recommends. "I recommend the Door Trail. It's not very long and has a boardwalk, but you can go beyond it and it really puts you into the badlands itself. The landscape you find yourself surrounded by is almost surreal, like you're on another planet. Cliff Shelf Trail is great as well. It has a little bit of elevation to it, but it provides spectacular views after you walk through the juniper forest. Because of the diversity on that trail, you have the opportunity to see some wildlife, and it's a great spot for birding. The fan favorite at Badlands is the Notch Trail, which has a wooden rung cable as a ladder that goes up to the side of a relatively steep part of the Badlands. This is a very common place for rescue efforts due to leg injuries, so be careful and, again, know your limits."

Badlands was the first national park Chris Zayas visited with her husband as newlyweds, back in the summer of 1983. "We drove from Illinois to the Badlands and I was fascinated at the changes in landscapes as we traveled. I was awestruck!" she remembers. "Nothing anyone could describe in words could have prepared me for the incredible sights as we drove through the park for my first time. It was like landing on the moon, and it was incredibly beautiful. One of the days we were hiking the Badlands, we came across a ranger who was excavating a site with a small fossil. My husband Bill has always loved dinosaurs and fossil hunting. The ranger asked if he wanted to help and let Bill use a brush to clear away some of the dirt."

Patrick Rodden, a photographer and national park lover, visited Badlands during a stormy week. "Two F1 tornadoes touched down in park boundaries along with a funnel that passed over my car," he shares. "As the rain was so heavy, it eroded the Badlands to the point fossils were rolling down the sides to the ground. The rangers incentivized children to find fossils, but not touch them, and come back to the visitor center to report their locations. The kids were then given prizes for locating fossils without disturbing them."

Guadalupe Mountains National Park
Texas

Southwest

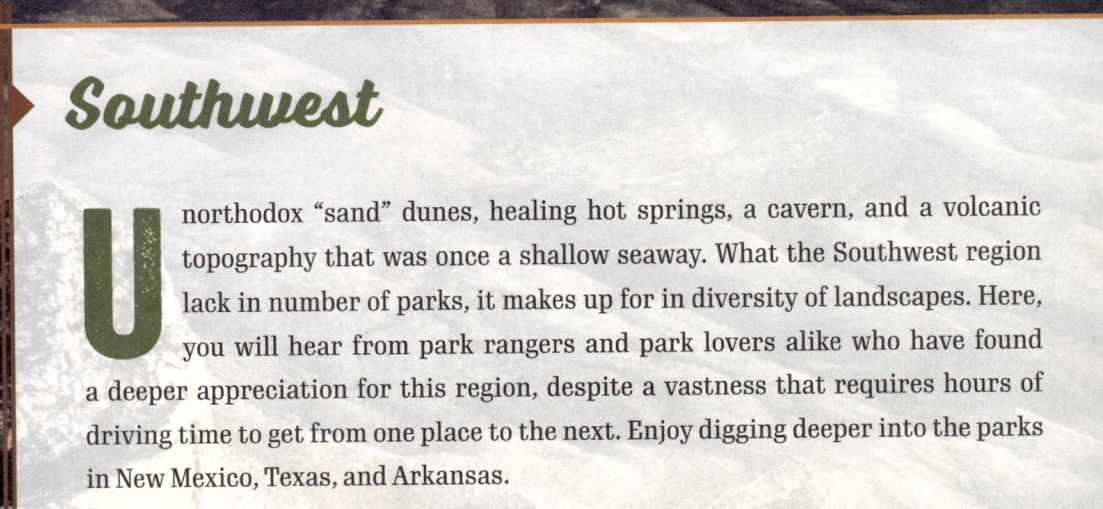

Unorthodox "sand" dunes, healing hot springs, a cavern, and a volcanic topography that was once a shallow seaway. What the Southwest region lack in number of parks, it makes up for in diversity of landscapes. Here, you will hear from park rangers and park lovers alike who have found a deeper appreciation for this region, despite a vastness that requires hours of driving time to get from one place to the next. Enjoy digging deeper into the parks in New Mexico, Texas, and Arkansas.

Southwest

Hot Springs National Park

Unconventional by park standards yet rich in cultural heritage, Hot Springs National Park is where history meets Mother Nature. Besides the historic bathhouses, the park conserves the thermal spring water and preserves the hydrological system that feeds the springs.

The idea of protecting water resources is what inspired Ranger Ashley Waymouth to become an environmental lawyer. She grew up in Laredo, Texas, near the Mexican border, with a dad who taught middle school history. Each year, he'd take a group of students to Washington, DC, New York, and Pennsylvania, so Ranger Ashley got to spend her spring break learning about US history from historians and park rangers.

"I graduated from college with a history and philosophy degree and began studying for the LSAT. I went to a river that flowed right through the middle of town to wait for the library [where the test would be held] to open," she recalls. "As I sat along the banks of the river, I was stunned by how clear the water was. I could see fish, I could count all the rocks that were over 10 feet down, I was mesmerized, and my mind flooded with questions; it was like a Pandora's box had opened in my mind and then it hit me. I took the LSAT but right

Thermal spring water emerges at 143°F. The water must be cooled before visitors enter it.

ESTABLISHED	LOCATION
1921	Central Arkansas
SIZE	**VISITATION NO.**
9 square miles	2,502,967
LAND ACKNOWLEDGMENT	
Ancestral land of the Quapaw Osage, and Caddo people	
FOR MORE INFO, VISIT:	
www.nps.gov/hosp	

before I turned in my scantron, I flipped it over and canceled my scores. From that moment on, I set out to learn everything I could about the natural world. I worked as an environmental educator for many years before becoming a park ranger."

Hot Springs National Park was once known as "America's Spa." Ranger Ashley shares that "the bathhouses that make up Bathhouse Row were instrumental in some of the advancements in medicine that we see in the nineteenth and twentieth centuries and stood as beacons of hope and healing for those who were sick, in pain, and suffering from 'incurable' ailments. The thermal springs emerge from the ground so hot that no pathogenic bacteria can survive in the water. The park maintains several jug fountains that dispense the untreated, unfiltered thermal springs water for all to enjoy."

Bathhouse Row consists of eight bathhouse buildings constructed between 1892 and 1923 along the Grand Promenade.

The park's visitor center is located inside Fordyce Bathhouse, which also houses a free museum. For a soaking experience, Ranger Ashley recommends the Buckstaff or the Quapaw Bathhouses. "Since the water emerges at 143°F, it is unsafe to get in without cooling the water down, which is why soaking is limited to the bathhouses. The park also has 26 miles of trails, many of which are interconnected, so it's the perfect place to 'build your own hiking adventure' and escape the hustle and bustle of downtown Hot Springs." You can also camp at the park's Gulpha Gorge Campground or opt for a luxurious stay at the historic Hotel Hale on the Bathhouse Row, which has large soaking tubs in each room that can be filled with hot spring mineral water.

TRAILBLAZING!

Hot Springs has been **protected as a reservation** since 1832 (before earning its national park status almost a century later), making it the oldest protected area within the National Park Service system.

Southwest

Carlsbad Cavern National Park

ESTABLISHED	**LOCATION**
1930	Southeastern New Mexico
SIZE	**VISITATION NO.**
73 square miles	394,121
LAND ACKNOWLEDGMENT	
Ancestral land of the Mescalero Apache people	
FOR MORE INFO, VISIT:	
www.nps.gov/cave	

Carlsbad Cavern is a limestone labyrinth that was formed when sulfuric acid dissolved the limestone, shaping the 119 caves (and counting!) that can be found underground. The Big Room, the Bottomless Pit, and the Natural Entrance are just some of the remarkable features of the park. Above ground, the Chihuahuan Desert provides a good alternative for foot exploration.

Ranger Nick Lashley is a true cave geek who is now living the dream as a cave guide at Carlsbad Cavern National Park. His interest in caves started in a cave closer to home: Mammoth Cave National Park, the first national park he visited. "My first trip into the world's longest cave was on a fourth-grade field trip," he remembers. "It was an eye-opening experience, seeing a place where animals like eyeless fish and shrimp could live. It felt like a whole other world. Growing up, we traveled through or by the park just about every Sunday afternoon visiting grandparents, aunts, uncles, and cousins. Some parts of my family lived there before it was a national park. The surface felt like home and the cave felt like an adventure."

Ranger Nick's ideal job is one where he can be outside (or in a cave) and not have to check his inbox. "I just wasn't sure how to materialize that," he says. "During my last year of university, I took a summer

The Natural Entrance Trail allows visitors to explore the cavern on their own pace.

course called Exploration of Mammoth Cave. For five days, an amazing team of current or former rangers took me and a handful of others through the historical progression of passages explored in the park. Getting a taste of the immensity and history of the cave was amazing, but learning more about the reality of a career in the national parks was the most valuable lesson learned. It was a tough day learning that park rangers still have to have emails, but seeing their office made me know that it would be worth occasionally sorting through an inbox."

The Big Room was the most beautiful thing Ranger Nick had ever seen, which still holds true today. "Carlsbad Cavern is a spectacle to behold. It routinely rewards the observant visitor," he says. "My favorite aspect is the supreme detail that you can spend a lifetime observing, studying, and enjoying." As a park ranger, Nick enjoys the deep relationships he's forming with such special places. "Showing up to work every day allows you the opportunity to see the resource in so many different lights," he explains. "The changing seasons, migrating wildlife, and guest fluctuations make for an engaging and dynamic insight into some of the world's greatest treasures."

While Ranger Nick loves a pedal-to-the-metal trip, he thinks it's important that visitors allow enough time to truly slow down and enjoy what they've worked so hard to see: "Try to spend more time experiencing the park than the time you took to travel there!"

The unique cave formations that continue to grow and decorate the cavern are formed by rain and snowmelt that soak through limestone rock and eventually drip into the cave below.

TRAILBLAZING!

From May to October, visitors gather at the **Bat Flight Amphitheater** near the Natural Entrance to Carlsbad Cavern before sunset to await thousands of bats making their daily exits from the caverns in search of dinner.

Southwest

White Sands National Park

ESTABLISHED	LOCATION
1933 (redesignated 2019)	Southern New Mexico
SIZE	**VISITATION NO.**
225 square miles	729,096
LAND ACKNOWLEDGMENT	
Ancestral land of the Mescalero Apache, Tampachoa (Mansos), and Piro people	
FOR MORE INFO, VISIT:	
www.nps.gov/whsa	

White Sands National Park is home to the world's largest gypsum dune field. (For contrast, most inland sand is usually silica.) It's believed that the park area was once under water, and gypsum was created at a higher rate than it could be dissolved in water. Once the water evaporated, the larger gypsum pieces broke into selenite, the crystallized form of the mineral gypsum, which is actually clear. As selenite further eroded by wind and weather, it looks white to our eyes.

White Sands got its name from the whiteness of its gypsum "sand."

As a park ranger at White Sands, Brian Powers enjoys helping visitors connect with the parks, both intellectually and emotionally, while creating experiences that will be remembered for years to come. His favorite story to share is about the evolution of the animals in the area. "Before the white sands were here, the landscape was much darker. As the gypsum dunes began to form, however, the landscape became more and more white," he explains. "Lighter animals could better match their white surroundings and were thus more likely to survive and reproduce. As a result, after about 7,000 years and thousands of generations of living here in the white gypsum sand dunes, many animal species are now a lighter color than their relatives living outside just a few miles away."

Since White Sands is a bit out of the way (and has limited cell phone coverage), Ranger Brian says, "The park is a place of wonder, inspiration, and beauty but it is important to safely enjoy the park to get the most out of your experience. Bring plenty of food and water. Fill

Slow-growing yucca on the sand dunes.

up water containers at the visitor center as there is no water available in the dunefield. It is important to know your limits when it comes to the difficulty of a physical activity, elevation, the heat, and the cold. Temperatures can drop very quickly once the sun sets or during storms. Exploring the outdoors comes with its risks. Our job is to work to reduce those risks, but your safety depends on your own good judgment, adequate preparation, and constant awareness."

My first trip to White Sands was before the park received its national park designation, during a multi-park road trip across Arizona, New Mexico, and Texas. Besides driving down Dunes Drive, an eight-mile scenic drive that starts at the visitor center into the heart of the gypsum dunefield, I hiked most of the trails at the park, such as Playa Trail, Interdune Boardwalk, and Alkali Flat Trail. Back then, I strived to hike at least one

TRAILBLAZING!

The sand at White Sands remains cool even in hot weather. Since the sand particle is **gypsum and not silica**, which absorbs heat, the white sand makes for a pleasant walk, especially in the summer.

strenuous-rated trail in each national park—Alkali Flat trail was it. Pro tip: Don't start a desert hike in the peak of the afternoon. (Yes, I did that at Death Valley too—see page 78.)

Alkali Flat Trail is a five-mile loop up and down the dunes. I came across two hikers during my hike,

Footprints in White Sands National Park.

a mom and her adult son who I learned were visiting from Wisconsin. I resumed my hike and had several more stop-starts along the trail to take in the scenery and capture photos, so the duo caught up to me and we continued our hikes almost parallel with each other. Once we got back to the trailhead and walked to our cars, the mom, Ana, shared that she was thankful our paths crossed earlier on the trail when I first spotted her and her son, since she was contemplating turning around. Seeing another soul on the dune attempting

Ripples in the sand.

the same hike inspired her to continue her journey. That is the magic that a park like White Sands creates: the opportunity to bond with other nature lovers who are just as passionate about the parks as I am.

This park is also a special one for me since it was the very first national park that I introduced my now-husband to. I had the trip to White Sands already booked to celebrate the new year and the national park designation, and we had only been dating for about a week when I invited him to come along. He booked a last-minute flight to Albuquerque, we made the almost four-hour drive to the park, and we spent the evening witnessing a magical desert sunset. We've visited twenty more national parks together since then, along with numerous other National Park Service sites.

A stunning sunset at White Sands National Park.

White Sands National Park
New Mexico

Southwest

Big Bend National Park

Santa Elena Canyon is one of the famous stops in Big Bend National Park.

Big Bend National Park is an unassuming place that includes the entirety of the Chisos mountain range and a large portion of the Chihuahuan Desert. With more than 150 miles of trails to explore, the park is a hiker's paradise. As you enter, you're greeted by a sky island, where the Chisos Mountain rises from the vast desert floor—a wild and rugged sight to behold.

Originally from India, dark sky chaser and photographer Kedar Halbe now resides in Austin, Texas. His first national park, however, was all the way in Maine, where Acadia set him off on his national park bucket-list journey. "Having lived mostly in urban areas for most of my life, I had never truly experienced a dark sky until Acadia," he shares. "The experience was transformative, and I realized that I wanted to keep experiencing things like these by being outdoors, hiking, camping, and laying back to watch the night sky."

An engineer by day and astrophotographer by night, Kedar loves experiencing the night sky at Big Bend. "It is quite a hike to get to Big Bend from Austin. I could get to some of the Arizona or Utah national parks (including flight and driving) in the same amount of time that it takes me to get to Big Bend. But that long drive is totally worth it. Buzz Aldrin described his first view of the moon as 'beautiful desolation.' I tend to think of Big Bend in those terms, far away from civilization

ESTABLISHED	LOCATION
1944	Southwest Texas

SIZE	VISITATION NO.
1,252 square miles	509,129

LAND ACKNOWLEDGMENT
Ancestral land of the Chisos, Mescalero Apache, and Comanche people

FOR MORE INFO, VISIT:
www.nps.gov/bibe

and one of those places where you can enjoy solitude and the beauty of nature, a beautiful desolation of sorts. I guess 'magnificent isolation' would be a more fitting description." Big Bend has the darkest skies in the contiguous United States. Kedar explains, "The park itself is in an internationally recognized dark sky reserve where special precautions have been instituted to prevent light pollution so you can experience brilliant night sky and see the Milky Way galaxy, the Andromeda galaxy, and other celestial delights such as constellations and nebulae." If you prefer to enjoy the park behind the wheel instead of on foot, Kedar suggests hitting the Ross Maxwell scenic drive, where you can catch several of Big Bend's iconic views along the way.

For photographer, hiker, and road tripper Andrew Fisher, the park holds a special memory. "I proposed to my now-wife in Big Bend. It was a fantastic evening on the South Rim of the park," he shares. "We enjoyed a horseback ride from one of the local towns and spent the night in a tipi near the ghost town of Terlingua. The next day, we backpacked to the South Rim to spend the night. We later watched the sun set over Mexico and I had my camera set up to capture the moment. Little did my wife know, I had a ring in my pocket and asked her to be my wife. It was a beautiful moment that tops all others."

TRAILBLAZING!

Big Bend is named after the big bend in the **Rio Grande** that flows through the park. Roughly 118 miles of the park's boundaries run along the international border between the US and Mexico.

The park boundary includes the entirety of the Chisos mountain range.

Southwest

Guadalupe Mountains National Park

When it comes to diversity, Guadalupe Mountains National Park takes the cake. Salt flats, fossilized reef mountains, grassland, stunning fall foliage amidst its maple-tree forest, and, most importantly, the highest summit in the state of Texas, Guadalupe Peak, can all be found here.

Ranger Theresa Moore's first national park was Acadia, when she was less than 10 years old. She grew up in the South and frequented beaches where the water was usually warm. "When we went to Maine and there's the ocean, my brothers and I went running into the water. We quickly turned around because the water was so cold!" she remembers. "We stopped and looked around, there was nobody in the water."

Her career as a park ranger started when she literally hiked into the job while visiting Zion. "I had just finished graduate school. My old roommate from college and I took a month to travel to all the national parks in the west. We went to Zion and did a guided ranger hike at the Emerald Pools," she says. "At the end of the hike, I asked the ranger, how can I do what you're doing? He says, 'Well, I'm short-staffed. Are you available for an interview tomorrow?' So I found myself the next day in my Chacos and shorts. They interviewed me, I gave them my resume, and that's how I got into the National Park Service."

ESTABLISHED	LOCATION
1972	West Texas
SIZE	**VISITATION NO.**
135 square miles	227,340

LAND ACKNOWLEDGMENT
Ancestral land of the Mescalero Apache people

FOR MORE INFO, VISIT:
www.nps.gov/gumo

The rugged mountain tops seen in the park today consist of marine fossil reefs uplifted from the Chihuahuan Desert floor.

The park's Nipple Hill at sunset.

For Ranger Theresa, one of her many favorite parts about Guadalupe Mountains is the ecology. "When you start hiking at the trailheads, you're starting down in the desert, which is still high at 5,600 feet in elevation, but it's absolutely desert. Everything has a thorn. Then you hike 3,000 feet up in elevation and you're in a ponderosa pine forest. Another interesting aspect of this park is its ties to 14 different Native American nations. For the Apache people, the Guadalupe Mountains are sacred. So you have to remember that, as well as that they have been here forever and this place is important to them."

To enjoy a safe visit to the park, Ranger Theresa says to check the park's website, do your research, and know your limits. "Just because we have the tallest peak in Texas doesn't mean that's the hike you have to do," she suggests. "We have amazing hikes that don't necessarily take you to the top of Texas, but will be stunning anyway. Read what the different trails have to offer and then find the trail that will give you the experience that you want in a national park. Most importantly, look at the weather and be prepared. And lastly, be flexible. If you find something beautiful, stop and enjoy it. That's going to be the moment that will stay with you. Think about how amazing it is that you found this spot, this area. Maybe it wasn't the end point of your hike, but for you, that was your summit, wherever you were going."

TRAILBLAZING!

Geologist **Wallace Everette Pratt** was instrumental in the creation of this park. He was introduced to Guadalupe Mountains by an associate during a business trip, fell in love with the area, purchased land, and later donated it to the National Park Service to be preserved.

Isle Royale National Park
Michigan

Midwest

The Midwest is home to some of the most underrated national parks in the country, including two recently redesignated national parks. The national parks in Missouri, Ohio, and Indiana are easily accessible to urban communities. Though some may argue that the views there aren't as iconic as the national parks you'd find out west, that opinion may be swayed after local park rangers share their fondest memories and best stories. As for the two parks up north near the Canadian border, you have to go beyond the visitor center and get on the water to appreciate the immense beauty and peacefulness that Michigan and Minnesota's national parks have to offer.

Midwest

Indiana Dunes National Park

ESTABLISHED	**LOCATION**
1966 (redesignated 2019)	Northwestern Indiana
SIZE	**VISITATION NO.**
24 square miles	2,765,892
LAND ACKNOWLEDGMENT	Ancestral land of the Miami, Peoria, Mahican, Mascouten, Meskwaki, Sauk, Shawnee, Kiikaapoi, Kaskaskia, Iroquois, and Potawatomi people
FOR MORE INFO, VISIT:	www.nps.gov/indu

Some people flock to Indiana Dunes for its beach, while others visit to recreate and be one with nature. Though it may not seem like it at a first glance, Indiana Dunes National Park is home to one of the most biologically diverse habitats in the country. The trails in this park will take you through multiple environments, from shoreline to sand dunes, to wetlands, prairies, river system, oak savannas, and beyond.

For local Indiana resident Bill Smith, who grew up 20 minutes down the road from Indiana Dunes, it was a surprise to learn that the park was just a stone's throw away. "The state park was my refuge as a little kid and especially in the teenage years, for socializing. When I got home from college and discovered that we had a national lakeshore (at the time) here, I wondered, how did I miss this? As a kid, I couldn't wait to grow up and get away from here to see some real nature like [what they have] out west. Then as I learned more about the dunes, I realized I needed to just stay here. I taught at different high schools in Indiana, Michigan, and in Chicago Public Schools in my 38 years of teaching. Being a seasonal park ranger at this park was my summer job starting in 1984, before I became a permanent ranger years later."

A former teacher of agriculture and science, it's not surprising that Ranger Bill loves the Chellberg Farm

The Dune Succession Trail highlights the four stages of dune development along its one-mile length.

The park was initially protected to preserve the sand dunes from industrial sand mining activities and steel company land purchases.

at Indiana Dunes. "My students and I used to raise the chickens and the turkeys there when we stayed at the farm in the summertime. We've had kids help get cattle there," he says. "It was a wonderful extension of my classroom." His second-favorite part of the park is the Pinhook Bog Trails System, which offers a rare ecosystem.

Ranger Bill and I share a favorite trail, the Dunes Succession Trail. "It's basically the reason why there's a national park here," he explains. "The research that Dr. Henry Cowles did with the plant succession is what put us on the map for preservation."

It's important to check the weather before visiting, especially in summer. "We have the tendency to irritate people that come to the beach at one o'clock on a 90-degree day, after driving two or three hours to get here, and once here, there's no parking spot," Ranger Bill explains. So either call ahead or arrive early! When there's no parking left, "the best strategy is to find a trail and hike a little bit further away from the lake where there's plenty of parking. Try to come back to the beach in mid-afternoon, before the sunset crowd shows up."

TRAILBLAZING!

Indiana Dunes was the birthplace of ecology. **Dr. Henry Cowles** studied the different types of plants that grew in the sand dunes and he concluded that the shape of land and the type of soil significantly influence the type of plants that grew there.

Midwest

Isle Royale National Park

Rugged, remote, and with zero vehicle traffic, Isle Royale National Park is worth the complex logistical planning and research. Located in Lake Superior, Isle Royale has over 450 islands, more than 160 miles of wilderness trails, and is known for its healthy moose population. The park has lower visitation numbers, but a high number of return visits for those who yearn for more (myself included).

Ranger Liz Valencia grew up in the Midwest and has been working at Isle Royale for over 30 years. She's a historian by training, which is how she found her way into the National Park Service. "My jobs have been in several resources management and history roles," she says. "Only in my mid-career did I switch and officially become a park ranger. I really like the variety of the job here. Part of it is because with the lake, you're never really sure what's going to happen from the day-to-day. Now I'm more into interpretation, so seeing that part through the visitor's eyes is fun. Talking to visitors and hearing what they like about it and seeing the excitement in their eyes when they show up on the boat, that's fun. I also like seeing that same excitement in the new staff every

Isle Royale was formed by igneous rock layers that folded as a result of tectonic plate movement.

ESTABLISHED	LOCATION
1940	Northern Michigan
SIZE	**VISITATION NO.**
893 square miles	28,965

LAND ACKNOWLEDGMENT
Ancestral land of the Ojibwe, Cree, and Assiniboine people

FOR MORE INFO, VISIT:
www.nps.gov/isro

TRAILBLAZING!

Gray wolves, the top predators at Isle Royale, have resided in the park since the late 1940s. It's believed that they crossed an ice bridge formed between the Canadian mainland and the island.

season when they start, especially if they've never been to Isle Royale before."

Her favorite part of the park is Lake Superior itself. "That's really the most intriguing part of the park. It influences everything that happens there," she explains. "I think it's an incredible body of water and our world is a pretty unique one, being out there and in the lake." One useful resource that the park curated is the first-time visitor's guide to Isle Royale, available on the park's website, which covers all the logistics to consider before embarking on an adventure. Ranger Liz also reminds visitors to be ready for any changes to conditions and be aware that they are all part of the Isle Royale National Park experience.

A visit to this park is usually centered on the largest island, Isle Royale, but your visit is your own—do what you like! If you're day-tripping it, spend some time walking around the island and find your way to the shoreline. If you're into miles on the trail, backpack or thru-hike along the Greenstone Ridge Trail that traverses the island. In the words of Ranger Liz, "Find a spot to be by yourself and immerse yourself in the island."

The park consists of over 450 islands within its boundaries.

Midwest

Voyageurs National Park

ESTABLISHED	**LOCATION**
1975	Northern Minnesota
SIZE	**VISITATION NO.**
341 square miles	220,825
LAND ACKNOWLEDGMENT	
Ancestral land of the Cree, Monsoni, Assiniboine, and Ojibwe people	
FOR MORE INFO, VISIT:	
www.nps.gov/voya	

With more than a third of the park consisting of bodies of water, Voyageurs National Park is best experienced out on the water. The four major lakes within the park boundaries are Rainy, Kabetogama, Namakan, and Sand Point. The park is named for the French-Canadian fur traders who voyaged through the region in the 1800s, but the Ojibwe people had been paddling the lakes for many, many years before that.

The first National Park Service unit that Erik Ditzler visited was Shiloh National Military Park in Tennessee, when he was six or seven years old. "I didn't know anything about the Civil War, but it felt like an important place," he remembers. "That trip is what ultimately led to my love of history. So I studied history in college but didn't initially use my degree. I visited a lot of parks, museums, and historic locations and eventually decided that I should be a park ranger."

Ranger Erik loves how unique Voyageurs is. "Almost everything is only accessible by boat in the summer, but you can trek across frozen lakes in the winter. The lakes are stunning, and the recreational opportunities are

Solitude and sunset make for a perfect getaway at Voyageurs National Park.

abundant," he says. "Every campsite is secluded. You may have an island to yourself! The night sky is very dark so you can see countless stars, and maybe even the northern lights. There are also lots of stories from people that lived here throughout the years, from the Ojibwe people, gold miners, lonely fisherman, and homesteaders."

Like many park rangers, Erik enjoys sharing stories and meeting people who are driven to find adventure. "I get to give advice on what they might enjoy seeing and experiencing," he says. "Working in a place that people take a once-in-a-lifetime trip to is very fulfilling! I sometimes see wolves on my drive to work, or discover something in the park library that motivates me to research a new topic. It is also very rewarding to have a small part in conserving America's treasured places and stories."

For your visit, Ranger Erik suggests, "Pick a nice, quiet spot to spend a night. Listen to the loons, gaze

One of the many lakes at Voyageurs.

at the stars, and dip your toes in the water. Also, don't be afraid to visit in the winter. It is a totally different experience. Take a snowshoe hike to a beaver pond or go cross-country skiing. Maybe try out ice fishing or snowmobiling in the backcountry." For those who aren't fond of kayaking or don't want to rent their own boat, you can join the ranger-guided boat trip in the summer. Some of the tour route travels a similar path to that taken by the voyageurs through Rainy and Namakan Lakes. Spend a few nights camping, or rent a houseboat in the summer for a unique experience.

TRAILBLAZING!

Voyageurs has **655 miles of pristine, undeveloped shoreline** and more than 500 islands within its boundaries. The park lies in a transition area between the southern boreal forest on the north side and temperate deciduous forest on the south side.

Midwest

Gateway Arch National Park

A view of the Old Courthouse from the top of the Gateway Arch.

Previously known as the Jefferson National Expansion Memorial, this urban national park commemorates Thomas Jefferson's vision and the role of St. Louis during the Westward Expansion. Gateway Arch National Park covers the iconic arch itself, the new and improved underground visitor center and museum, the Mississippi riverfront, the green spaces and trails, and the Old Courthouse located directly across from the arch.

Born and raised in St. Louis, it's no surprise that Gateway Arch was Pamela Sanfilippo's first National Park Service unit. It also happens to be where she works now. "We didn't do much traveling to visit national parks when I was young," she says. "It wasn't until I was finishing grad school that I had the opportunity to work as a seasonal park ranger at Ulysses S. Grant National Historic Site. I hadn't ever considered this as a career path, but once I started that first summer, I had the bug!"

Though Gateway Arch is the smallest of the designated national parks, the park is rich in history, covering 200 years of important civil rights stories.

Best of all, it's an incredibly accessible park. Ranger Pam explains, "Being in downtown St. Louis presents great opportunities for civic engagement and helping diverse audiences that typically would not be able to visit a national park to enjoy 'their' park. I love sharing the stories related to the park and helping people find their own connection to the past. I also think it is great to share that the parks belong to everyone. While the

ESTABLISHED	LOCATION
1935 (redesignated 2018)	Eastern Missouri
SIZE	**VISITATION NO.**
0.14 square miles	2,422,836
LAND ACKNOWLEDGMENT	
Ancestral land of the Kiikaapoi, Kaskaskia, Osage, Myaamia, and O-ga-xpa people	
FOR MORE INFO, VISIT:	
www.nps.gov/jeff	

The monument took two years to construct and is made of stainless steel. Gateway Arch is as tall as it is wide.

National Park Service is responsible for caring for these places, it's so important to help visitors know that they too can be stewards of the parks. Working with students who typically haven't seen themselves at the parks is so rewarding."

Ranger Pam says it's best for summer visitors to make reservations for the tram ride to the top of the arch ahead of time, due to peak crowds that time of the year. At the top, you get a 360-degree view from 630 feet above the city. Ranger Pam also enjoys the North Gateway, "one of the hidden gems," which is part of the over five miles of hiking and biking paths in the park. "It is a real oasis in the city," she says. The Old Courthouse, where Dred and Harriet Scott first sued for their freedom in 1846, in a case that would end up in the US Supreme Court in 1857, is part of the park. At the time of writing, the Old Courthouse is undergoing renovations to make the historic structure more accessible and to add new state-of-the-art exhibits. It's anticipated to reopen in mid-2025.

TRAILBLAZING!

The **arch** is the tallest artificial monument in the United States. It is 630 feet tall and 630 feet wide at its base. An engineering marvel, it weighs over 43,000 pounds and was designed to withstand an earthquake.

Midwest

Cuyahoga Valley National Park

ESTABLISHED	LOCATION
1974	Northeast Ohio
SIZE	**VISITATION NO.**
51 square miles	2,860,059
LAND ACKNOWLEDGMENT	
Ancestral land of the Iroquois, Mohawk, Munsee, Shawnee, and Lenape people	
FOR MORE INFO, VISIT:	
www.nps.gov/cuva	

If I were to describe Cuyahoga Valley National Park in a few words, I'd call it "an underrated urban gem." Although the views may not compare to the Grand Canyon, Grand Prismatic Spring, or the Tunnel View in Yosemite, this park has a lot to offer along the meandering Cuyahoga River (which was once on the EPA's naughty list). Its proximity to the surrounding urban communities makes the park accessible to many. In fact, it's one of the few national parks where you have cell phone coverage while hiking!

Rebecca Jones has been with the National Park Service for over three decades, with the majority of those years spent in Cuyahoga Valley. Starting in the freelance and non-profit world, she realized that she needed to pursue higher education to make ends meet. She then became a high school teacher, teaching biology before landing a summer gig working as a park ranger at Mammoth Cave. "When I was a kid, my parents took me to a state park in Kentucky. We went on a ranger-led program there and it blew my mind that the park ranger doing the program was a woman," she shares. "I remember thinking, a woman can do this? Mind you, this was back in the '70s. That was probably one of the first seeds planted for me to join the National Park Service. I've had the grace to work for a number of women who

The Beaver Marsh is among the most diverse natural communities in the park.

Cuyahoga Valley National Park
Ohio

Indigo Lake, originally the site of a quarry, is now a popular fishing location.

were groundbreakers in the NPS in their own ways. At times, it's not been exactly the journey I expected, but overall, it's way more than what I expected."

Weaving various American stories into the fabric that shapes our nation today is what energizes Ranger Rebecca, especially showing how these stories connect visitors to the nation. "For example, if you go into the Peninsula area in the park, it looks very much like a New England village, because the area was initially settled by New Englanders. Finding a way to connect the visitor to the area, or finding out somebody has an interest in transportation or railroad stories, I love that moment when people pause and you can just see the wheels are turning, that they had not thought of something that way before. Some park rangers call it the 'aha' moment."

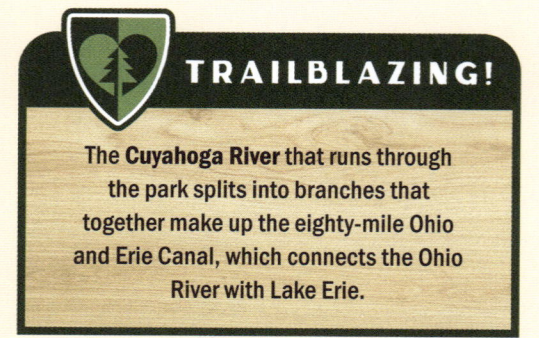

Unlike most other national parks, you can decide to visit Cuyahoga Valley on a whim, without extensive planning. Ranger Rebecca suggests that you start your visit at one of the park's visitor centers to get the latest

TRAILBLAZING!

The **Cuyahoga River** that runs through the park splits into branches that together make up the eighty-mile Ohio and Erie Canal, which connects the Ohio River with Lake Erie.

scoop for the day. "Maybe it's a day when we know there's a lot of water flowing over Brandywine Falls, or there's been a spotting of a tricolored heron at the Beaver Marsh, or the bald eagles are nesting at Station Road. If you stop at the visitor center, we can tell you what's going on that day in terms of our programs, and 'warn' you about what you might find that day. Just the other day, somebody saw a big snapping turtle at the Beaver Marsh."

The Brecksville-Northfield High Level Bridge runs through the park, connecting Brecksville with Sagamore Hills Township.

The Ledges Trail circles a plateau of towering wall rock formations and provides stunning views along the way.

There are many ways to enjoy the park, but for Ranger Rebecca, the waterfalls are her muse. My personal favorites are the Ledges and the Blue Hen Falls. Hiking the 1.8-mile Ledges loop takes you along towering rock formations covered in moss—a dream for a geology geek like me. Seeing the Blue Hen Falls during peak fall season is worth hiking the rugged Buckeye Trail. Another unique activity that you can do here is taking the two-hour National Park Scenic Excursion with the Cuyahoga Valley Scenic Railroad. The train travels between Akron and Peninsula, with multiple stops in between. If you wish to hike, bike, or kayak one way, you can always take the train back to your starting point. I highly recommend the opportunity for slow travel, as it allows you to soak in more of the scenery.

Cuyahoga Valley National Park
Ohio

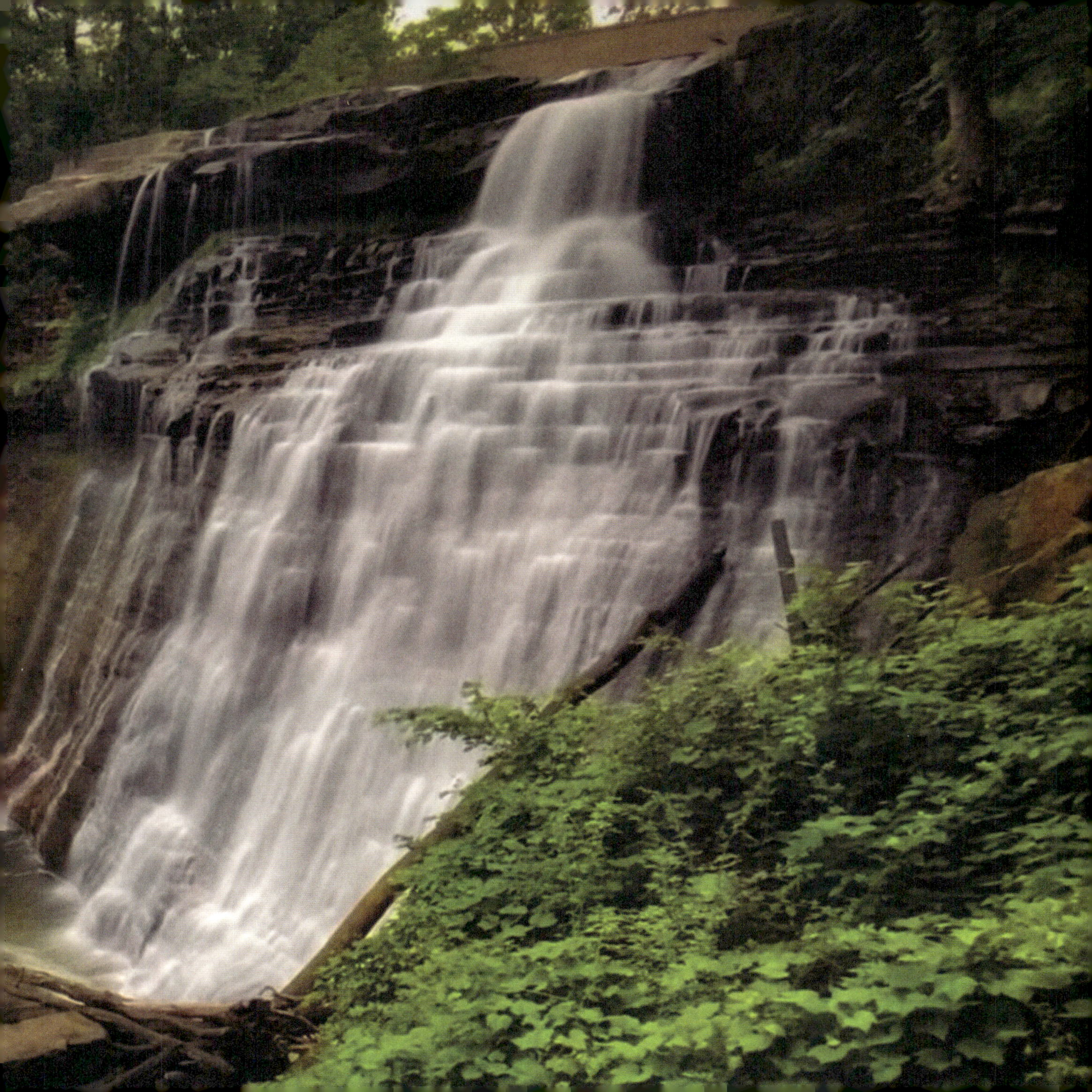

Great Smoky Mountains National Park
North Carolina and Tennessee

Southeast

If you think the Southeast region is predominantly filled with swampy landscapes, think again. In national parks across Florida, and a US territory in the Caribbean islands, you'll find turquoise open water and tropical reefs. If water isn't your muse, try the parks in Tennessee, North Carolina, South Carolina, and Kentucky, amongst the rolling hills of the Smokies, under the cypress canopy in the floodplain forest, or underground in the world's longest known cave system. The stories you'll hear from these park's rangers and fellow national park lovers are sure to inspire.

Southeast

Biscayne National Park

ESTABLISHED	**LOCATION**
1968 (Redesignated in 1980)	Florida Keys
SIZE	**VISITATION NO.**
270 square miles	571,242
LAND ACKNOWLEDGMENT	
Ancestral land of the Tequesta, Taino, and Seminole people	
FOR MORE INFO, VISIT:	
www.nps.gov/bisc	

When visiting this watery wonderland, get ready to trade your hiking boots with water sandals or snorkel fins—this park is 95 percent water! Visit and be rewarded with clear turquoise water and a big sky full of fluffy clouds.

Having grown up in South Florida, Ranger Gary Bremen is used to having sand sticking to his feet. He attended a ranger program at White Sands National Park (monument at the time) in New Mexico as a seven-year-old boy, burying his feet into that special sand and wondering why it didn't stick to them like the Florida sand did. He was fascinated by the idea of how similar and yet how different parks across the country, big and small, could be, connected by a synergy that fit together to tell a much bigger story.

Being a ranger at Biscayne National Park meant taking care of the place that he grew to know so well as a child, and having the opportunity to help other people get excited about the place so that they too would have an appreciation of it and want to protect it. One of his favorite parts of the job was introducing visitors to things they didn't know prior to their visits. Most young visitors want to learn about manatees, turtles, sharks, dolphins, and occasionally pirates. But they come away knowing about the violet sea-snail (*Janthina janthina*), which floats on the ocean surface and devours Portuguese man o' wars when it bumps into them.

According to Ranger Gary, who spent over 30 years as park ranger at Biscayne, "pick your activity before

A palm tree in Biscayne National Park.

planning the timing of your visit." Despite its Floridian location, the park is multi-seasonal, so you can't do everything in every season. Winter and early spring are ideal for camping at the Keys to skip the mosquito and hurricane season. If snorkeling is your thing, I recommend a guided tour with Biscayne National Park Institute to explore the Biscayne Maritime Heritage Trail.

There's more to this park than the admittedly Instagram-worthy Boca Chita lighthouse. Jones Lagoon is a personal favorite of both Ranger Gary and I, though for different reasons. For him, it's where he married his husband. "I love the upside-down jellies at the bottom of the lagoon and the surrounding mangroves tree," he shares. As for me, it was where I had my first experience doing some standup paddleboarding, albeit sitting down for the most part.

While there may not be hundreds of miles of hiking trails, Biscayne is a great place for you to enjoy the slow pace and take in the coastal views. "I was standing on top of the lighthouse, just me and another guy," Ranger

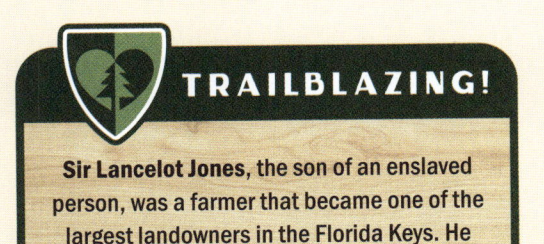

The Boca Chita Lighthouse in the park.

Gary recalls. "We saw a turtle and watched it for quite a long while, and nobody else knew the turtles were there because other visitors just go to the top of the lighthouse and walked right back down. Be on the lookout for the little things and appreciate them, as it's not always about the giant charismatic megafauna."

A "Grand Slam" day at Biscayne National Park is when you get to see the big four: manatees, turtles, sharks, and dolphins. Also take the time to become a Reef Ranger and earn your park patch! This program was curated by the park staff with the help of two national park lovers, Sandra and Evan, to provide an opportunity for visitors to learn more about the coral reef there. But above all, to ensure a memorable visit at a park that is challenging to explore on foot, Ranger Gary says, "trust the experts—park rangers genuinely want to help you enjoy the place that they love." If you're planning a visit to Biscayne, check out the Heritage Cruises with Biscayne National Park Institute. Ranger Gary guides the tour every Monday as part of his retirement gig.

TRAILBLAZING!

Sir Lancelot Jones, the son of an enslaved person, was a farmer that became one of the largest landowners in the Florida Keys. He later sold his lands to the NPS for the creation of Biscayne National Park.

Southeast

Dry Tortugas National Park

ESTABLISHED	LOCATION
1935 (redesignated 1992)	Florida Keys
SIZE	VISITATION NO.
100 square miles	84,285
LAND ACKNOWLEDGMENT	
Ancestral land of the Seminole people	
FOR MORE INFO, VISIT:	
www.nps.gov/drto	

There's more to the Florida Keys than Key West. Despite its name, Dry Tortugas is the wettest national park in the country, with 99 percent of the park area being water. Accessible by ferry or float plane from Key West, this park is perhaps one of the easiest to plan in comparison to other "remote" parks.

Originally established as Fort Jefferson National Monument, this was the first park Ranger Curtis Hall ever visited while growing up in Key West. Who would've known that, after serving a decade in the US Navy and then finishing his undergraduate degree, that he would end up back at his very first park, working as a park ranger.

"After traveling all around the globe with the navy and to be able to come back and work at the very first park that I ever came to as a kid was pretty much a dream come true," Ranger Curtis says. "To top it off, working on youth education programs and to be one of our national park divers—it checked all the boxes. I like to say that this park is a confluence of human history, natural resources, and scientific discoveries. From the first early Spanish explorers and their guide from the Calusa tribe, to seabirds nesting, growing in size and abundance whereas in other parts of the United States and Caribbean Basin the same species are declining in

Fort Jefferson was built to protect one of the most strategic deepwater anchorages in North America.

The park is home to about 30 species of coral. The reefs harbor a rich and colorful diverse marine life such as fish, sponges, sea stars, and anemones.

numbers, and the most ambitious coastal fortification that the country ever created, built by the enslaved African Americans at the time, which later turned into a prison. Even to this day, the stories are ongoing. Earlier in 2023, we had over 300 Cuban migrants land over the course of two or three days. That's what I mean. It's a blend of human history and natural resources that you just don't find at all other parks."

Besides working with students, Ranger Curtis also works with a wounded veterans' group through a national program called Wounded Veterans and Parks. "We had a group of eight gentlemen out last year, three of which were Purple Heart recipients and had some pretty significant disabilities," he says. "We did multiple dives with them to do some buoy work and bleach surveys. I took one of the veterans on a coral reef diving tour of the *Windjammer* wreck, a ship the size of a football field that went down in the early 1900s. At the end of the dive, he looked at me and said, 'That was better than any prescriptions the VA's ever given me.' Those are things that I enjoy."

Ranger Curtis recommends doing three things at Dry Tortugas: walking down the beach by Bush Key (only open September to mid-February), going to the fort to get pictures from the top tier overlooking Loggerhead Key and underneath the arches, and snorkeling by the historic cooling docks in the South and North Beach.

TRAILBLAZING!

The "dry" in this park's name refers not to the amount of water, but the **lack of fresh water** on the island. "Tortugas" refers to the **turtles** observed by Ponce de Leon and his crew when they first arrived.

Southeast

Everglades National Park

Cypress domes are mostly found in and around the park and the neighboring Big Cypress National Preserve.

Close enough for a day trip from Miami, yet far enough to be immersed in nature, surrounded by the largest tropical wilderness in the United States, the subtropical wetland ecosystem of Everglades National Park spans 2,000,000 acres, protecting the remaining 20 percent of the original Everglades in Florida. As far back to the 1800s, the landscapes of the region have been altered by humans through water diversions and flood-control structures, restricting flow of water across critical areas.

Everglades was the first national park that Evan Wexler, an educator, photographer, and national park lover, visited at the age of three. It is his "home park" and he visited multiple times throughout his childhood. "I was always a 'nature kid' and I loved being outside and learning about animals and the environment. The Everglades was perfect for that, as it's one of the few national parks created to preserve biodiversity and not just the landscape," Evan says. "Those early visits to Everglades gave me a foundation for understanding and appreciating our public lands. National parks are landscapes where long-held dreams come true."

Both American alligators and crocodiles can be found in the Everglades.

ESTABLISHED	LOCATION
1947	Southern Florida
SIZE	VISITATION NO.
2,410 square miles	810,189
LAND ACKNOWLEDGMENT	
Ancestral land of the Seminole, Miccosukee, Calusa, Tequesta, Taino, Jega, and Ais people	
FOR MORE INFO, VISIT:	
www.nps.gov/ever	

TRAILBLAZING!

The largest intact stand of **protected mangroves** in the Northern Hemisphere thrives in the Everglades' tidal waters, where freshwater from the Everglades mixes with saltwater from the ocean.

Ranger Gabriel Curbelo had a similar experience: "I grew up right on the shores of Biscayne National Park. It's a place that has been important for me and my family for generations as a source of recreation and retreat from the hustle and bustle of the city. My journey to becoming a park ranger began by volunteering at Zoo Miami. As a result of partnership between the zoo and the National Park Service, I had the opportunity to be trained in interpreting about the Everglades in preparation for a new exhibition at the zoo." That's how he met the Director of Education for Everglades. "Later on, while in college, I received an announcement for an internship to work for the education program at the park. I was hired in 2019 and became a park ranger in 2021," Ranger Gabriel shares.

Everglades was founded for its biological diversity rather than the traditional geological wonders of the American West. "When visiting the park, it can be very hard to see what a remarkable place it is," Ranger Gabriel says. "Rangers like to say that this place 'whispers to us.' Over time, I went from seeing the park as a hot and humid place to a home for the many plants, animals, and indigenous people of South Florida. We get visitors from all over the globe wanting to learn about the Everglades."

Ranger Gabriel has several recommendations for your Everglades bucket list, such as the wet walk (or slough slog, as the park named it) in winter, because, "It is such a special experience to enter a Cypress Dome and see just how clean and clear the water is." If getting in the water doesn't appeal to you, another great stop is the Marjory Stoneman Douglas Wilderness Waterway, to enjoy the true nature of South Florida.

The warm and shallow swampy water of the Everglades has attracted all types of birds to this region for thousands of years.

Southeast

Mammoth Cave National Park

ESTABLISHED	LOCATION
1941	Central Kentucky
SIZE	**VISITATION NO.**
83 square miles	654,450
LAND ACKNOWLEDGMENT	
Ancestral land of the Cherokee, Shawnee, and Chickasaw people	
FOR MORE INFO, VISIT:	
www.nps.gov/maca	

With more than 400 miles of chambers and rock tunnels, Mammoth Cave is home to the longest cave system known in the world. It's also one of the oldest tourist attractions in North America, dating back to 1816 after the saltpeter mining operation there ceased. More than a century later, a movement to protect the park was initiated by private citizens, eventually leading to the national park designation.

The park is home to thousands of years of human history and a rich diversity of plant and animal life.

Ranger Molly Schroer went to school at Western Kentucky University, majoring in recreation. Part of the program required her to put in some volunteer hours, which led her to discover Mammoth Cave, where she eventually interned as a cave guide for the summer. "I had graduated from college and at the end of my season I thought, *What do I do next?*" she says. "The people I worked with said to apply at other national parks. That's a great way to see the country and different cultures that I wasn't exposed to growing up in Indiana."

Experiencing Mammoth Cave for the first time shaped Ranger Molly's view of what she wanted to do with her career. "I have a very fun job here where I get to do special events and communications initiatives on things we have going on. It's fun to work in a place where

The flowstone cave feature hangs downward, creating draperies, as notably displayed by this Frozen Niagara example.

people are on vacation," she says. "One of my favorites is when you're in the cave with a tour and you hear the reactions for the first time as people round the corner and that cold cave air hits them, or they're descending down the historic entrance into this big beautiful hole in the ground and people are just in awe . . . Especially the kids, who get very excited when they go into a cave."

Ranger Molly recommends booking your cave tour online before your visit to ensure you get the one you're eyeing, especially during the busy summer season. "A good basic introduction to Mammoth Cave is our classic Historic Tour," she says. "It goes in our big historic entrance and passes through the Big Open Canyon passageways. The second half goes down deeper into the lower passages where the rooms become very small. One of my favorite tours is the Violet City Lantern tour, where we don't turn on any of the electric lights. It's a three-mile, three-hour tour, but you get to see the cave by lantern light. It's really neat to see the shadows, hear the stories, and see how they originally explored the cave back in the early 1700s."

TRAILBLAZING!

Mammoth Cave's oldest passage is thought to have formed between **10 and 15 million years ago**, when water from surface rivers and streams seeped through cracks into underground rock beds. The passages are still actively forming today.

Southeast

Great Smoky Mountains National Park

Straddling North Carolina and Tennessee is one of America's oldest mountain ranges, named for the morning fog that hangs among the peaks. Great Smoky Mountains National Park is a favorite for many rangers and fellow park lovers, and it was actually the most-visited national park for many years.

It's impossible not to find joy in a place as stunning as the Great Smoky Mountains. Such was true for Brad Ryan and his grandma, Joy Ryan, the dynamic duo that spent the last eight years traveling across the country visiting all 63 national parks. "This was the trip that really started it all for us," Brad shares. "It's my attempt to fulfill my grandma's lifelong dream of seeing her first mountain. I contacted her while I was in my fourth year of vet school and asked her how she felt about it. She said, 'What time are you picking me up?' We drove through the night to Elkmont campground. That was the night that she slept in a tent for the very first time. She fell off the air mattress twice! We laughed the entire time. The next morning, it was still raining but by the early afternoon, the fog lifted and the rain stopped. We hiked 2.5 miles up to the Alum Cave Bluffs and everybody that we met along the way greeted us at the top with a round of applause."

In a park as big as Great Smoky Mountains, there are many ways to enjoy the outdoors. Try to spot black bears driving around the Cades Cove, where I've had luck (and so have Brad and Joy). The famous Appalachian Trail also runs through the Smokies for 72 miles. Brad and Grandma Joy have done several trips along the trail. But another favorite memory for them in Great Smoky Mountains National Park was walking up to Clingmans Dome to take in the view of the mountain range painted in autumnal colors. That was the moment that inspired Brad to invite his grandma on their whirlwind adventure that has taken them to all 63 national parks.

"From my perspective, oftentimes we leave the elderly behind because we make assumptions about their capabilities," Brad says. "What I found through my experience with Grandma Joy was that the national parks

ESTABLISHED	LOCATION
1934	North Carolina-Tennessee border
SIZE	**VISITATION NO.**
816 square miles	13,297,647
LAND ACKNOWLEDGMENT	
Ancestral land of the Cherokee people	
FOR MORE INFO, VISIT:	
www.nps.gov/grsm	

Great Smoky Mountains National Park
North Carolina and Tennessee

Great Smoky Mountains National Park
North Carolina and Tennessee

offered her new inspiration in life and new opportunities to get stronger, healthier, and happier. Her balance and coordination improved by taking one step at a time on the trails. We want to show the world that there are accessible trails like the Trail of the Cedars in Glacier, scenic drives and cruises like the Jenny Lake cruise in Grand Teton, and activities like whale-watching off the coast of Ventura on your way to the Channel Islands. National parks are for people of all ages and we want to make sure that other people who are in their 70s, 80s, or even in their 90s like Grandma Joy see themselves reflected in that diversity of the national parks."

Great Smoky Mountains also won Ranger Rebecca Jones's heart. Although she has spent the last two decades working at Cuyahoga Valley, she goes back to the Smokies any chance she gets. For her, going to the mountains is going home. "My parents had been going to the Smokies since before I was born. I love walking

Laurel Falls in Great Smoky Mountains National Park.

out into those mountains and just being," she explains. "Listening to the sounds, the wind, the animals, the water, the trees moving, or sometimes, depending on how the day is flowing, maybe there's silence. There's some centering and some grounding going on there because we often get so caught up in everything we're doing all the time during the days that we don't take that moment. So there's something about those mountains. That is one [park] that I truly, truly love."

TRAILBLAZING!

This park is the **Salamander Capital of the World**, home to 24 species of lungless salamanders. Often found near creeks and under rocks, they absorb oxygen and release carbon dioxide through the walls of blood vessels in their skin and the lining of their mouths and throats.

Great Smoky Mountains National Park
North Carolina and Tennessee

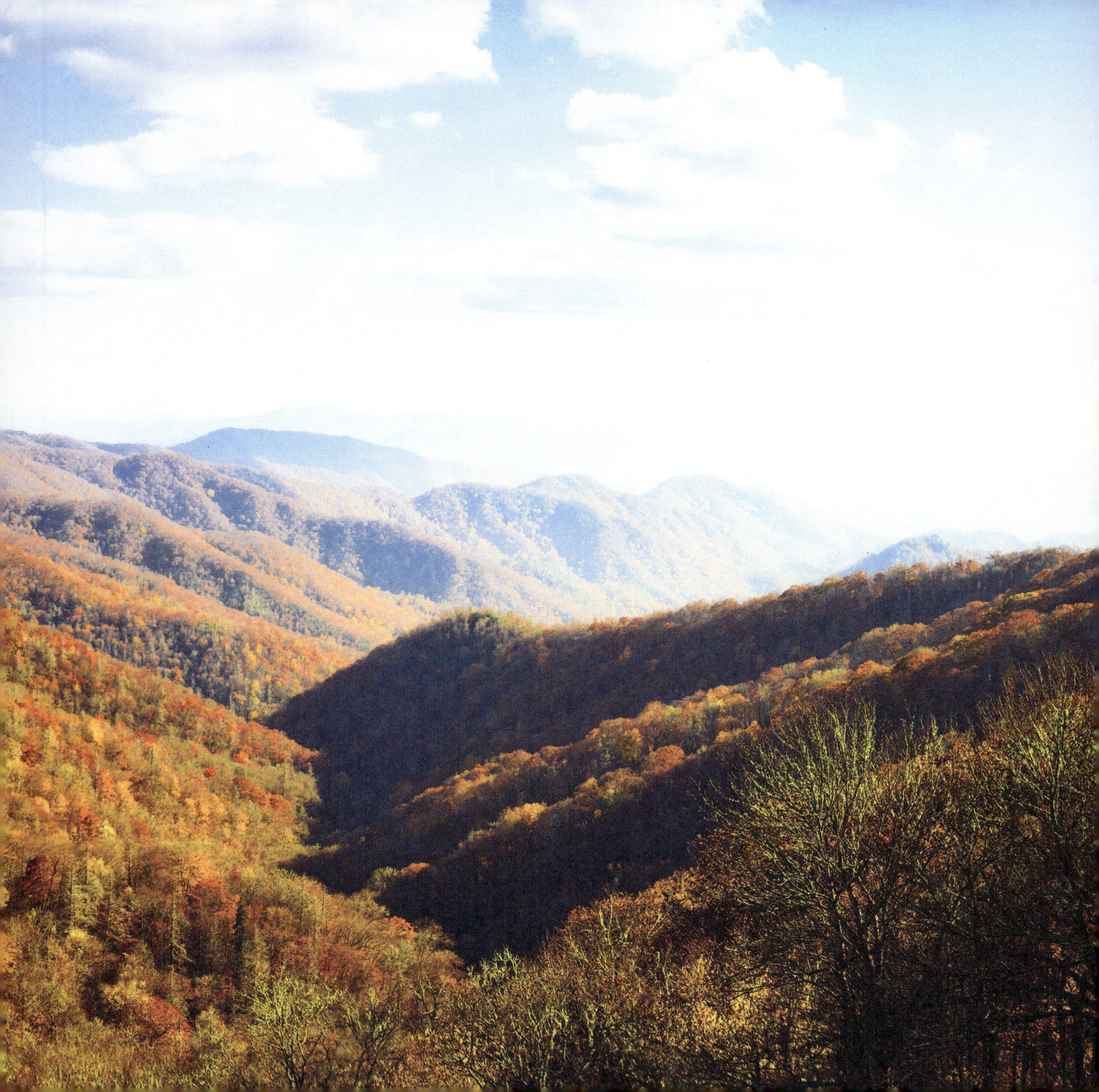

Southeast

Congaree National Park

ESTABLISHED: 1976 (redesignated 2003)

LOCATION: Central South Carolina

SIZE: 41 square miles

VISITATION NO.: 250,114

LAND ACKNOWLEDGMENT: Ancestral land of the Congaree people

FOR MORE INFO, VISIT: www.nps.gov/cong

Congaree National Park is geographically located in a floodplain that often floods during wintertime, so it is often incorrectly considered a swamp park. It was first established to protect the last swath of old-growth bottomland hardwood forest remaining in the United States. Nicknamed the "Redwoods of the East," the Congaree forest is the tallest in eastern North America.

Patrick Rodden, who photographs his way through the parks, grew up 30 minutes from Congaree. It was his very first national park, back when it was known as Congaree Swamp National Monument. "Congaree is pretty special because I have visited it with many friends and family members. I became friends with a park ranger, and a local naturalist through my visits."

Patrick appreciates how the national parks serve to educate visitors on a multitude of topics. "I understand there is divisive history in the parks that is currently being rectified, brought to light, and shared by the National Park Service. But in that respect, they have the opportunity to shed light on America in its rawest form," he explains. "Within the bracket of the

Congaree preserves the largest area of old growth bottomland hardwood forest left in the United States.

The Cypress "knees" are thought to provide air during flooding or to serve as anchors over the root system.

TRAILBLAZING!

The **rich soil** in this region made for a great settlement, but the **hardwood forest** also provided refuge for escaping enslaved men and women. Those who didn't make the long journey north formed the maroon community in the woods.

park system, history and nature unravel to tell the story of our treasured public lands. The more parks I visit, the more I realize how embroiled in history each of us is as a citizen. Our story—the good, the bad, and the ugly—is told at a scholarly and academic level in the national parks. It's a department that represents the diversity of the country through its representation of units and its workforce."

For Patrick, his greatest memories of Congaree are taking walks with family and friends under the loblolly pines and the bald cypress trees, because "I have shared Congaree with many people who are important in my life. I have also had the opportunity to enjoy it through the eyes of naturalists, rangers, and enthusiasts. I think I have seen Congaree in about every season and weather event other than snow, and I have been on hikes at all times of the day from pre-dawn to full moon. Congaree is brimming with life, and you can always expect to see animals on hikes."

My favorite memory from Congaree is canoeing down Cedar Creek with my now-husband. The river passes through a primeval old-growth forest and is filled with diverse wildlife along the banks. Halfway through paddling, our guide pulled us over to the bank so we could explore the ground and walk amongst the cypress knees.

The Boardwalk Trail is a great introduction to the park, where visitors can experience the wilderness and solitude of Congaree.

Southeast

Virgin Islands National Park

The Virgin Islands are home to stunning white-sand beaches and over 3,000 years of human history.

One might argue that any time is a good time to visit Virgin Islands in the Caribbean. The ocean and sunshine make it perfect for swimming with sea turtles, snorkeling over coral reefs, hiking in the tropical forest, and visiting historic sugarcane plantations. The best time to visit Virgin Islands National Park is any time outside hurricane season (September to November), to lessen the risk of weather-related changes of plan.

My first time in Virgin Islands National Park, I went there on a whim. I had a plan for the weekend that got canceled and I needed a new one, pronto. At the time, I only had eight parks left on my national park bucket list, so Virgin Islands was an easy pick. During my visit, I squeezed everything I could into a three-day weekend. I stayed at an Airbnb in Southside, on St. Thomas Island, right in the middle of the island and on the water by Bolongo Bay.

On the first day, I drove to Charlotte Amalie ferry terminal to head to Cruz Bay. I made it to the visitor center just before they closed, then walked to Lind Point trailhead to hike up to the overlook. It started raining during my hike back down and I worried I'd slip down the muddy trail—only to end up slipping down the trail anyway (I had the entire 12 seconds recorded on my phone!). Next day, I took the vehicle ferry from Red Hook to Cruz Bay and

ESTABLISHED	LOCATION
1956	The Caribbean
SIZE	VISITATION NO.
23 square miles	343,685

LAND ACKNOWLEDGMENT

Ancestral land of the Taino (Arawaks), Kalinago (Carib), Ciboney, and Igneri people

FOR MORE INFO, VISIT:

www.nps.gov/viis

There are three species of turtles inhabiting the waters of St. John. They spend most of their lives in the water and only come to shore for nesting.

explored the island by stopping at some of the trickier spots, a little off the beaten path, while I had my rental car. On my last day, I took the passenger ferry from Red Hook to Cruz Bay and traveled within the park via the shared taxi available, getting on and off at multiple attractions.

One of the days, I did a kayak and snorkel trip with Virgin Islands Ecotours. I happened to be the only person who signed up and luckily it didn't get canceled. I hiked from the visitor center to Honeymoon Bay and met my guide there. My guide and I paddled out to Henley Cay, a small, uninhabited island that's part of the national park. After securing our kayak on the shore, we headed into the ocean. It was only my second time snorkeling and I wasn't a strong swimmer, but the thought of traveling all that way without getting into the water motivated me to conquer my fear. Although there were not many coral reefs in the water at the time due to the damage caused by the last hurricane, I was rewarded with the experience of swimming with a sea turtle, a stingray, and a couple of other colorful fish.

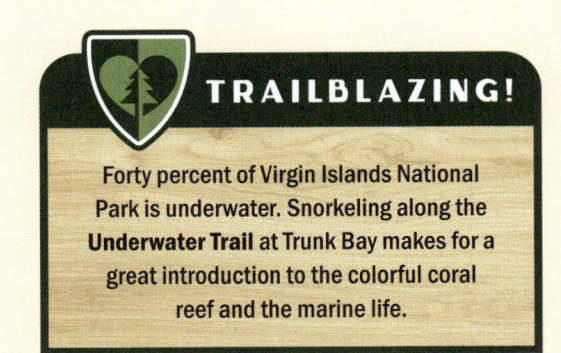

TRAILBLAZING!

Forty percent of Virgin Islands National Park is underwater. Snorkeling along the **Underwater Trail** at Trunk Bay makes for a great introduction to the colorful coral reef and the marine life.

New River Gorge National Park
West Virginia

Mid-Atlantic

In the mountain ranges in the Mid-Atlantic region, you will find some of the oldest building blocks of the United States. Valleys, rivers, ridges, and gorges are made even more beautiful when peak fall foliage appears on the many trees. The latest designated national park—found in West Virginia—is included in this region, as well as a wilderness escape in Virginia, for those looking to break away from the hustle and bustle of big cities. The story of human history at both parks dates back centuries, starting with its first inhabitants, prior to the settlement and industrialization, and continuing with the recreation and preservation in action today.

Mid-Atlantic

Shenandoah National Park

ESTABLISHED	**LOCATION**
1935	Northern Virginia
SIZE	**VISITATION NO.**
311 square miles	1,576,008

LAND ACKNOWLEDGMENT: Ancestral land of the Iroquois, Shawnee, Catawba, Cherokee, Delaware, Susquehannock, Manahoac, Monacan, and Massawomeck people

FOR MORE INFO, VISIT: www.nps.gov/shen

Virginia is for lovers, and so are our national parks! Spectacular vistas, cascading waterfalls, and stunning fall foliage are some of the things to love in Shenandoah National Park. Trade the asphalt of DC sidewalks for more than 500 miles of hiking trails, including 101 miles of the famous Appalachian Trail.

The North Mount Marshall summit is easily accessible from Skyline Drive. It's a short half-mile trip one way that leads you to an outcrop with expansive views.

The first time I visited Shenandoah was on a long weekend in 2017 with my best friend, Nazlin Shakir, who lives in New York. We drove from DC and arrived at the park as the late-afternoon fog rolled in. After pitching our tent at the campsite and connecting with two other park loving friends, Faizan and Melania, we went to catch a glimpse of the Shenandoah sunset. The next day, we scrambled up Bearfence Mountain for a quick jaunt.

Several years later, Nazlin would return to Shenandoah with her now-husband, where they got to witness the Milky Way with their naked eyes for the very first time. Her husband, Bryan Dinello, recalls, "At first glance, it looked like a cloud; but we were thrilled to discover that the 'cloud' was really the outline of our galaxy! The sky was a blanket of stars and it made us feel like tiny specks in the universe."

In her younger days, Ranger Margo Roseum taught her neighbor's kids about the constellations and exploring the outdoors. She spent a lot of time in and around Cuyahoga Valley National Park as a camp counselor in high school, and then landed a seasonal park ranger job there. "I worked for three summers as an interpretive ranger and one spring as an educational ranger in Yellowstone, spending my winters guiding tours. I worked for a summer in Olympic before moving east to Shenandoah. The spark I felt being outside from a young age and the joy I felt teaching others about my interests inspired my career path and I have loved it!"

Shenandoah National Park is over 100 miles long, so there's plenty to do. Ranger Margo says, "There is a lot of history to be discovered at the visitor centers, Massanutten Lodge, Rapidan Camp, and even along the trails and roadways. I enjoy long trails, when I have the time to dedicate, because they may have less people on them. While we do not have any lakes, there are dozens of streams and rivers that offer reprieve from the hot days or a relaxing day of fishing (just be sure to plan ahead and learn the regulations)!"

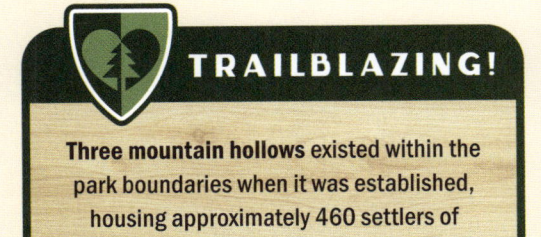

TRAILBLAZING!

Three mountain hollows existed within the park boundaries when it was established, housing approximately 460 settlers of European descent. It's believed the residents lived simple lives in log cabins, away from wider society.

A good stargazing spot in the park is by the Big Meadows area near the Rapidan Fire Road.

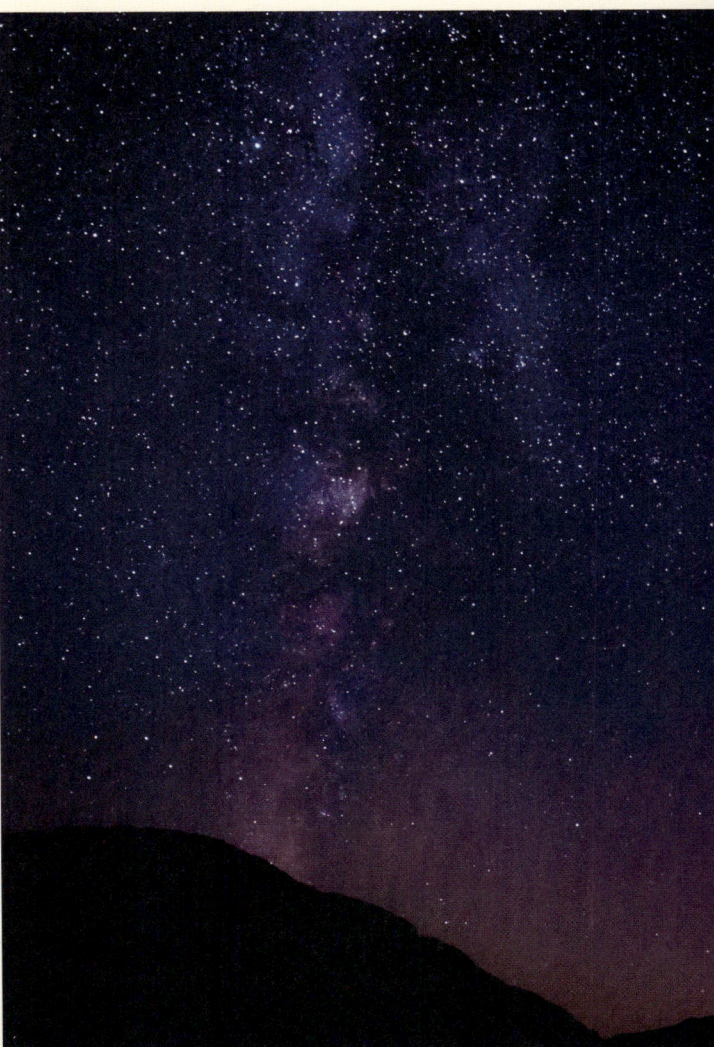

Mid-Atlantic

New River Gorge National Park

ESTABLISHED	LOCATION
1978 (redesignated 2020)	Southern West Virginia
SIZE	**VISITATION NO.**
114 square miles	1,707,223
LAND ACKNOWLEDGMENT	
Ancestral land of the Eastern Band of Cherokee, Tutelo, Yuchi, and Moneton people	
FOR MORE INFO, VISIT:	
www.nps.gov/neri	

Welcome to the 63rd national park of the United States, designated as such in 2020. Here, the views are gorge-ous and the river is, contrary to its name, one of North America's oldest, created between 10 million and 360 million years ago. The iconic New River Gorge Bridge is an engineering marvel, the third-longest single-arch bridge in the world (at the time of writing).

When she was a teenager, Ranger Eve West worked at the concession store for Buffalo National River in Arkansas. It was a convenient option, considering she grew up and lived right next to it. That was her exposure to the green and gray uniform, as rangers frequented the store. Her connections with that park led her to a

Take in dramatic scenes from the Main Overlook at Grandview.

The Endless Wall Trail provides hikers with great views of the New River almost 1,000 feet below.

TRAILBLAZING!

The completion of the **iconic bridge across New River** solved a logistical challenge, reducing a 40-minute drive down the narrow Fayette Station Road crossing the river into a less than a minute drive.

seasonal role there before she landed a permanent position with the National Park Service.

Today, Ranger Eve has been at New River Gorge for over a decade. She loves connecting with the visitors to share stories about the park, feeling that she has inspired them to look at things in a different way and promote stewardship. "I love working with the kids and helping them appreciate what they have here in their backyard," she says.

"Between the coal-mining, timber industry, and railroading industry, we have a lot of different stories," Ranger Eve explains. Carter G. Woodson, the man who sparked the idea that led to Black History Month being established, was a coal miner there. Henry Ford leased the town's Nuttallburg mines to have coal for his steel mills. "Mother Jones was right here in New River, fighting for workers' rights, and tried to establish unions in West Virginia for the coal miners," Ranger Eve adds. "[The diversity] is what makes New River one of the most unique places I've ever worked. It's also a meeting ground for a lot of plants that don't extend farther south or north. We have a tremendous biodiversity here."

If you're coming a long way to get to New River Gorge, plan to spend a minimum of three days. "There's a lot of places to check out here and we are surrounded by a number of state parks and two other smaller national park sites as well," Ranger Eve says. "Great restaurants, a lot of fun cultural things to do in the area. If you're looking for a quieter, more solitary experience, then Bluestone National Scenic River next door is

New River Gorge National Park
West Virginia

definitely the place you'd want to go to. As far as the view goes, Grandview is one of your best places. It's the highest point, top to bottom in the park."

Before I started visiting national parks religiously, I used to travel to big cities and be drawn to bridges—it's the engineering nerd in me. New River Gorge checks off a lot of things on my geeky list like hiking along the vertical sandstone walls that rim the gorge on Endless Wall Trail (and enjoying the local geology), strapping on a harness and doing the "bridge walk" underneath New River Gorge Bridge, white-water-rafting down the New River, and driving down Fayette Station Road in the evening as the fog rolls in to take in the view of the bridge.

One of my biggest memories at this park is taking my two friends, Brandi Small and Tammy Shakur, white water rafting for their first time. We booked a small cabin in Fayetteville as our base camp and went with the camp host for a half-day raft on the New River, also sharing the raft with a family that was celebrating the son's high school graduation. I had my phone out to capture the moments and the mom kept trying to tell me to put it away. As someone who has spent a week rafting down the Colorado River, hitting some Class 8, 9, and 10 rapids, I was well prepared for our New River experience. Plus, I had to capture the joy in Brandi's and Tammy's faces when they experienced their first rapid!

By the end of the trip, the mom asked me to send her some of the pictures and videos I'd taken. I share this to encourage you to find your joy and experience the park your way—as long as you stay prepared, keep safety in mind, and obey park rules.

New River Gorge includes 53 miles of the free-flowing New River, providing opportunities for water recreation such as river-rafting and canoeing.

Acadia National Park
Maine

North Atlantic

Though the North Atlantic only has one designated national park—in Maine—you can also appreciate the diverse historical parks and monuments located in the greater region. In this last national park of the book, you have the opportunity to catch the first sunrise in the nation (during winter and spring) in the "Crown Jewel of the North Atlantic Coast". In fall, experience the iconic New England changing leaves, just in time to enjoy the last few remaining sunny days and the magnificent show that Mother Nature puts on before winter comes around.

North Atlantic

Acadia National Park

Fall foliage in New England is stunning! Be sure to put it on your bucket list.

Established as a national park by private land donations, Acadia is where the ocean meets the mountains along a craggy granite coastline. Rich in cultural history, the park boasts hundreds of miles of hiking trails, and historic motor and carriage roads.

Sarah Olzawski visited Acadia National Park in the summer and experienced several days of heavy fog—unusual for that time of the year. "On my last full day in the park, I hiked Ocean Path," Sarah says. "I started in the fog at seven o'clock in the morning and as I made my way along the coast, the sun started to emerge and suddenly the park was dancing with color. It was like the moment in *The Wizard of Oz* when the camera switches from black and white to color. I was in awe at all the different greens and blues in the water."

Acadia was Mick Dees's first national park visit, and Patrick Rodden's last in the contiguous United States on his journey to see all 63 national parks. For Mick and Patrick, fall is when the magic happens. Patrick recalls being treated to "colorful leaves, rough seas, fog, and rain; each an aspect of New England that makes autumn perfect." Mick enjoys the crispiness of the air as winter approaches, and the many shades of the trees.

For Ranger Amanda Pollock, her very first national park site was the Minute Man National Historical Park in

ESTABLISHED	LOCATION
1916 (redesignated 1919)	Coastal Maine
SIZE	**VISITATION NO.**
77 square miles	3,879,890
LAND ACKNOWLEDGMENT	
Ancestral land of the Wabanaki people	
FOR MORE INFO, VISIT:	
www.nps.gov/acad	

230

Sunrise at Newport Cove in Acadia National Park.

Acadia National Park
Maine

Massachusetts. She remembers vividly the interactions she had with the park rangers, whether in uniform or dressed up in historic clothing for ongoing events. But it wasn't until an internship with the National Park Service during college that she realized she had found her calling. "I was initially drawn to the NPS because of the diversity of sites the agencies helped protect. I could put my history degree to good use at one of the many historical parks across the country, or I could work at a more traditional national park," she says. "What has made me stay with the NPS is the people. I work with some of the most dedicated people in the country. Their passion for their work inspires me every day, and that's a big part of why I can confidently say park rangers have the best job in the world."

To Ranger Amanda, the best part of Acadia is the people, from park staff to partners and those in the neighboring communities. "It's always wonderful to see how many people understand the power of this place, and how they come together to ensure we can preserve and protect the park for future generations," she says.

In Acadia, witnessing sunrise atop Cadillac Mountain is a special view to catch, especially from late fall to spring when you can experience the first sunrise in the continental US. Ranger Amanda is a fan of watching the sunrise along the scenic Ocean Drive, which begins at the park entrance station. And she believes that there's a trail for everyone in Acadia: "If I'm taking friends out for a quick jaunt who are not big hikers, the Wonderland Trail gives you a stunning view

The view from Acadia's North Bubble.

with a very easy walk. Great Head Trail is another great, relatively straightforward hike for people who want a little elevation gain. Just make sure you are hiking it on a dry day, as the granite cliffs can get very slippery!"

Acadia is often very busy, especially from spring to fall. Parking can be challenging, so Ranger Amanda's pro tip is to use the fee-free Island Explorer bus to get around the park. One important thing to remember for this coastal park is that the weather can be unpredictable, so proper gear is key to a safe and enjoyable visit.

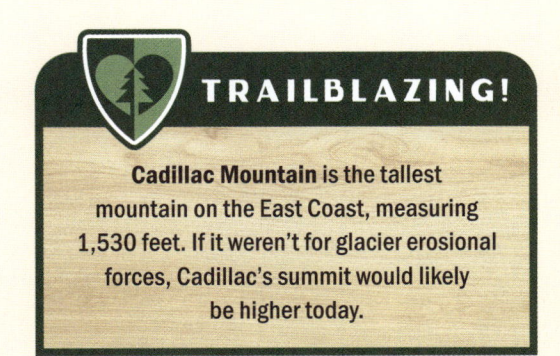

TRAILBLAZING!

Cadillac Mountain is the tallest mountain on the East Coast, measuring 1,530 feet. If it weren't for glacier erosional forces, Cadillac's summit would likely be higher today.

Acadia National Park
Maine

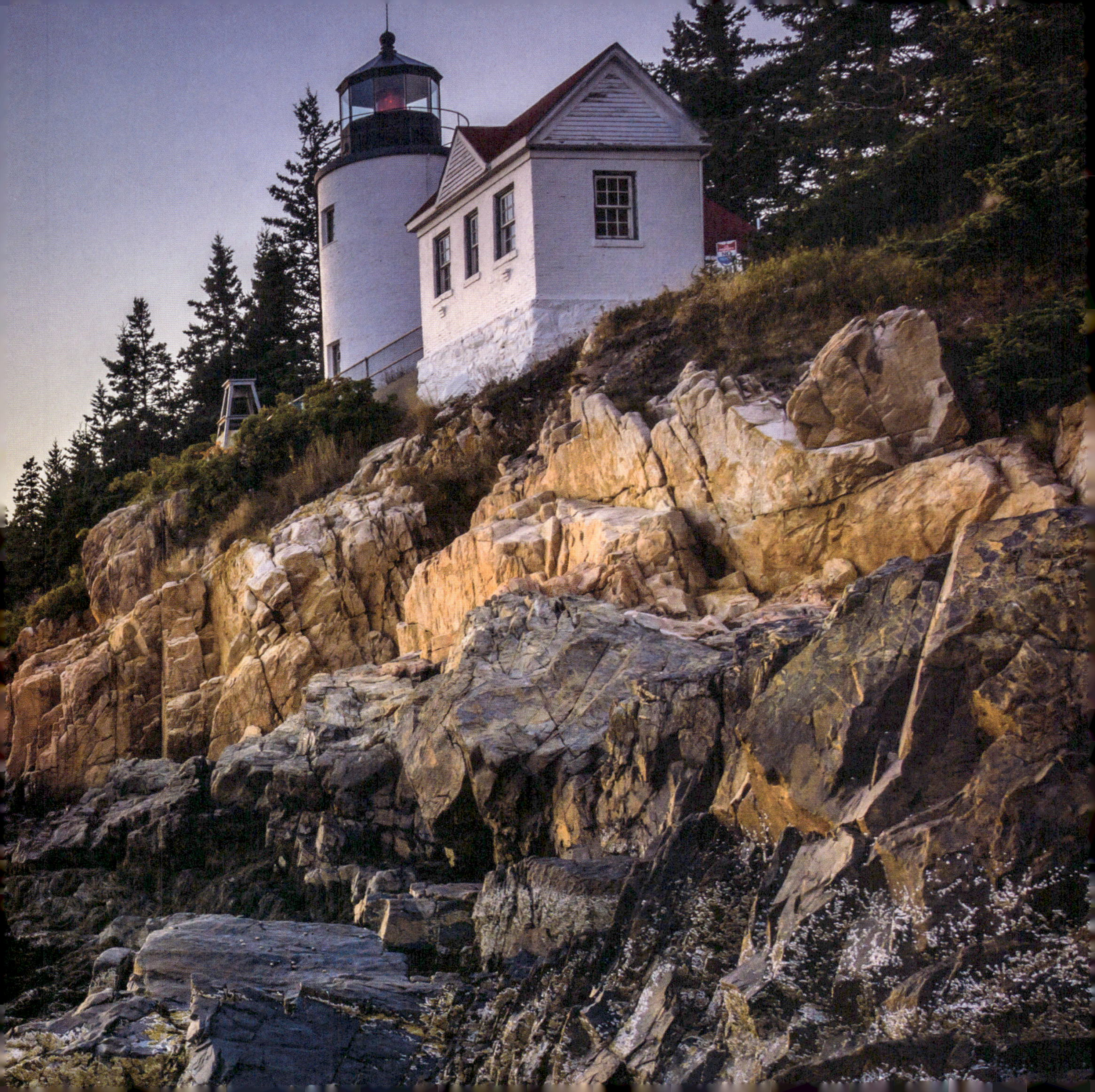

Beyond the 63 National Parks

Now that you've gotten to know all 63 designated national parks through the sights and stories curated in this book, let's shift gears and touch upon the "small parks." These 300-plus parks (and counting!) of various designations, alongside the 63 designated national parks, shape the fabric of America. The history, the people, the places, are unique to each site, but together they tell a more complete story of this country.

To Ranger Steve Phan, the Chief of Interpretation at Camp Nelson National Monument in Kentucky and the son of refugee parents, these small parks carry a big significance. "I was born in the US but my family is from Vietnam. One of the big things about the Civil War that I learned from the NPS came when they started really highlighting the experience of people of Asian descent that served in the US military during the war," he says. "My family served in the Vietnamese Civil War, so I got to learn more about where my family came from and the journey of a lot of people from across the Pacific. Camp Nelson being a refugee site during the Civil War and my identity as the son of refugees—this is in a way very personal."

"The relevancy of our parks, I think, is critically important," Ranger Steve continues. "You might not be a Civil War enthusiast, but you can come to Camp Nelson and learn about the experience of refugees, or of women that were trying to escape enslavement and trying to find their role in a country that was not affording rights to women, especially to African American women. Take some time to visit these 'small parks,' you're going to find a lot of meaning, and I hope inspiration as well."

Wupatki National Monument
Arizona

For Superintendent Chris Collins, who oversaw Ste. Geneviève National Historical Park in Missouri, one of America's latest small parks, the fun part of running a small park is getting to go behind the curtain every day. "It's a lot of work but protecting America's treasures is rewarding!" Superintendent Chris says. "One of the criteria for our park units is national significance. Each one is important to the story of our country and highlights something special that we decided is important to preserve and protect. On the surface, Ste. Geneviève has an apparent theme of French colonialism. When you scratch the surface, you see that it's so much more. One of my favorite historical figures connected to the park is Pélagie Amoureux. She was born enslaved but managed to secure her freedom and live with her family in one of the houses now owned by the National Park Service." Today, Chris Collins serves as the first superintendent of the New Philadelphia National Historic Site in Illinois. It's a newly established small park under the care of the National Park Service, commemorating the early nineteenth-century Black pioneers in that state.

Amanda Bauler and her family love small parks that allow them to explore history right where it happened. Some of their family favorites are George Washington Carver National Monument (such an incredible person), Canyon de Chelly National Monument (the views will leave you breathless), and Chaco Culture National Historical Park (where else can you camp within view of 1,000-year-old Ancestral Puebloan ruins?). To date, they have visited three-quarters of the 400-plus park units. For Bobby Beaulieu and his family, the president's birthplaces or houses are amazing places to experience hands-on learning of American history. They've learned numerous interesting facts about each president from those visits.

Devils Tower National Monument
Wyoming

Bobby also enjoys visiting forts. "There are so many forts across the country, from different periods of time, built by the Spanish, the British, the Revolutionaries, to the early Americans, and so on. It's hard to even compare forts amongst each other. And a place like Manzanar National Historic Site, we've visited three times and holds a special place in our hearts. When I first visited 10 years ago, I learned an entirely new narrative to World War II that I'd never known before. [It motivated me] to take my children to more park sites, to have these types of experiences and insight into history."

Although Tigran Nahabedian may have started his national park "career" as a Junior Ranger at Channel Islands National Park, a lot of his favorite park memories were made as a volunteer for the National Park Service and the first Buddy Bison Student Ambassador, a program sponsored by the National Park Trust. "I was invited by the National Park Service to help develop the National Digital Junior Ranger Experience at Fort McHenry in Baltimore," Tigran explains. "Unfortunately, there wasn't sufficient funding for my travel, so I raised money and helped sponsor and guide two busloads of students on their first visit to the park. I will never forget the excitement and enthusiasm these kids expressed during their visit, and I was overjoyed that they looked up to me as inspiration for their future adventures. I am proud to say that I have spent more than half my life advocating for equitable access to our public lands. I love national parks, but the Junior Ranger Program gave me a goal and often helped us plan what to do in the park. Some places, like the Statue of Liberty, Fort McHenry, and the National Mall, are symbols of our nation as much as our flag, while others, like Manzanar, are a grim reminder of the consequences of allowing our values to falter."

Love Your Parks

After journeying across almost 300 National Park Service sites over the last eight years, I can attest that these parks are indeed America's Best Idea. Though my national park bucket list started small, with only the nine California national parks and the desire to hike and learn more about Earth history (because geology rocks!), it later grew into seeing all 28 California National Park Service sites, when I became invested in learning about the human history of America, especially of the Indigenous People. The bucket list then evolved into experiencing all 63 national parks. I hope I'll get the opportunity to experience all 400-plus of the National Park Service units one day.

    These visits gave me new and deeper perspectives about this land that I didn't know much about prior to my time at the parks. From a personal perspective, my journey to these parks, be it as a solo traveler or with friends, has been pivotal to my growth as a person. The hours spent catching flights or miles driven from home to the remote parks, and the solitude found when on a trail early in the morning when everyone is still asleep in their tents or hotel rooms, have been so important for me. The time I made for myself, prioritizing "me time" and immersing myself in nature; noticing that my racing thoughts seemed to slow down on the trails; being in the moment, with my only goal to make it from Point A to Point B and back safely—these experiences have changed me for the better.

    As an immigrant myself, I think that going to the National Park Service sites is the best way to see and experience America. Not just for the sightseeing and the pretty vistas, but also the learning, and instilling a sense of appreciation for the land and a need to preserve nature and history. Whether you're a new or a seasoned traveler, a student, a family with kids, a retiree, or an aspiring (junior) ranger, there's something for everyone waiting in these parks. It doesn't always have to be a grand adventure hundreds of miles from home; it could simply be a stop at the Klondike Gold Rush National Historical Park while you're visiting Seattle, or a short drive to César E. Chávez National Monument near my home in California to learn about the critical civil rights figure who fought for the farm workers in the region. There are plenty of parks around you, big and small, ready to welcome you.

Folks, it has truly been a privilege to take you through this journey from Alaska to Maine, with all the states and territories in between. The stories, cherished memories, and words of wisdom from park lovers who work at or visited the parks have served as a tremendous inspiration and motivation for me to keep spreading my joy and passion for our parks with others. I invite you to go find your parks, whether it's one of the big 63 parks or any number of small parks that may be in your backyard. And most importantly, love your parks, share them with friends and loved ones, and recreate responsibly.

Miles and smiles, all the way!

César E. Chávez National Monument, California

Yosemite National Park
California

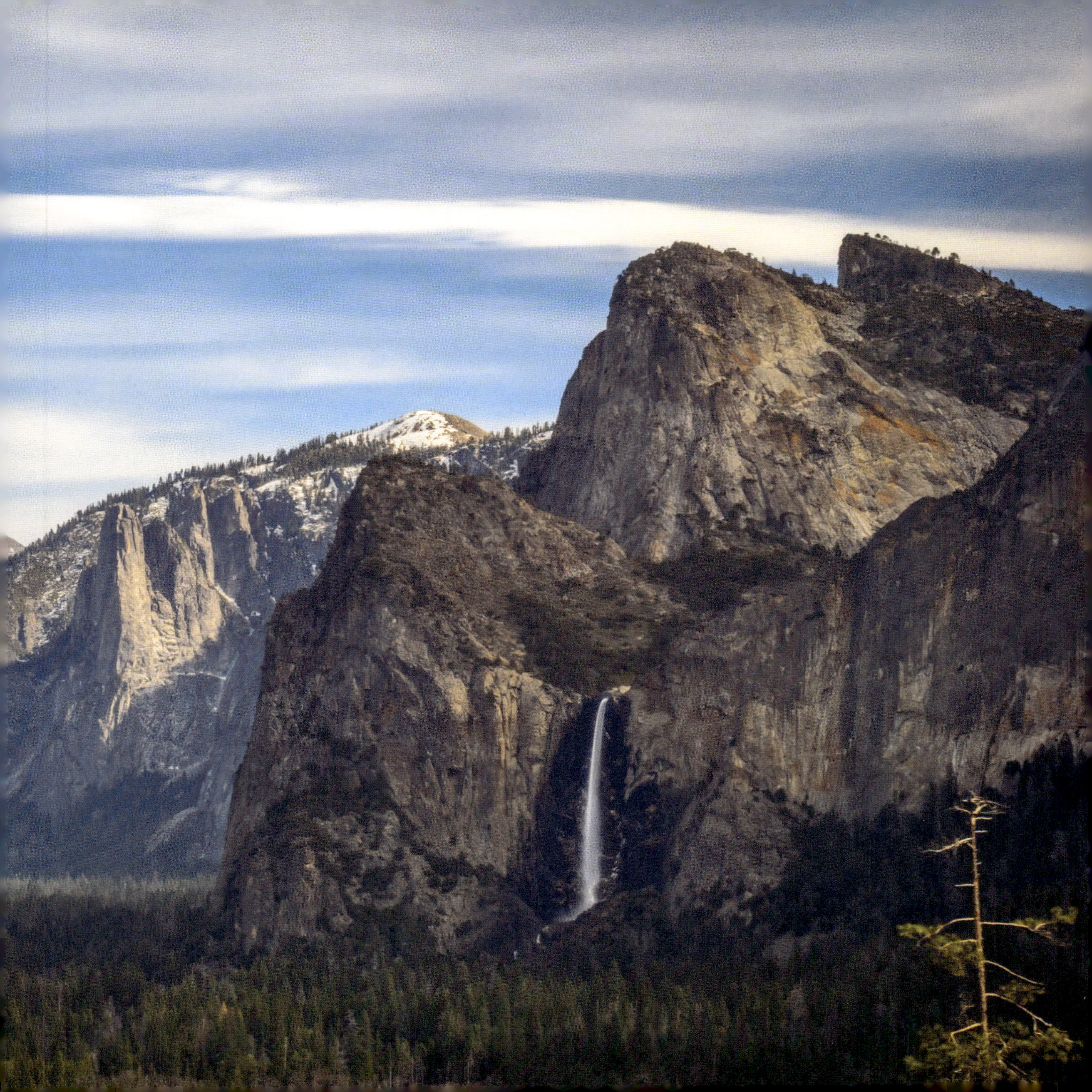

Resources

WEBSITES

- National Park System (400+ Units/Parks List): www.nps.gov/aboutus/national-park-system.htm
- Find a Park: www.nps.gov/findapark/advanced-search.htm
- Find a National Park Service Map: www.nps.gov/planyourvisit/maps.htm
- Plan Like a Park Ranger: www.nps.gov/aboutus/news/plan-like-a-park-ranger.htm
- Park Reservation and Timed-Entry Systems: www.npca.org/reports/know-before-you-go
- Annual Events at the Parks: www.nps.gov/subjects/npscelebrates/annual-events.htm
- Recreate Responsibly: www.nps.gov/planyourvisit/recreate-responsibly.htm
- Find Your "Virtual" Park: www.nps.gov/subjects/npscelebrates/find-your-virtual-park.htm
- Telling All Americans' Stories: Publications on Diverse and Inclusive History: www.nps.gov/articles/publications-diverse.htm
- Plan like a Park Lover: https://www.theparkschannel.com/
- National park adventures, travel tips, and logistics guide: www.thebucketlisttraveler.com

BOOKS

- *The National Park Bucket List: The Ultimate Adventure Journal for All 63 Parks* by Linda Mohammad (yours truly!)
- *Your Guide to the National Parks* by Michael Joseph Oswald
- *Moon USA National Parks* by Becky Lomax

NATIONAL PARK SERVICE SOCIAL MEDIA

- Facebook: Receive updates, news releases, photos, videos, events, and live streams from parks and NPS programs. Share your park photos, videos, and experiences with them and the rest of the national park loving online community. **www.facebook.com/nationalparkservice**
- Instagram: Get your daily inspiration of photos, videos, and live stories from parks around the country. **www.instagram.com/nationalparkservice/**
- Twitter: Receive park updates, news releases, photos, and videos from @NatlParkService. **www.twitter.com/natlparkservice**
- Flickr: Discover high quality, full-resolution public domain images. **www.flickr.com/photos/nationalparkservice**
- LinkedIn: Learn about internships, careers, and working with the National Park Service. **www.linkedin.com/company/national-park-service/**
- YouTube: Explore videos about wildlife, history, events, trip planning, and more. **www.youtube.com/nationalparkservice**
- Search individual national parks by name on social media to find and follow them!

**Grand Canyon National Park
Arizona**

▸ Credits

1. Amanda Pollock, Public Affairs Officer, Acadia National Park
2. Karen Garthwait, Acting Public Affairs Specialist, Arches & Canyonlands National Park
3. Aaron Kaye, Supervisory Park Ranger, Badlands National Park
4. Gary Bremen, Retired Interpretive Park Ranger, Biscayne National Park
5. Lori Rome, Chief of Interpretation & Public Information Officer, Black Canyon of the Gunnison National Park
6. Peter Densmore, Visual Information Specialist, Bryce Canyon National Park
7. Cadence Cook, District Interpreter, Canyonlands National Park
8. Shauna Cotrell, Visitor Services Program Manager, Capitol Reef National Park
9. Nick Lashley, Cave Guide, Carlsbad Caverns National Park
10. Ethan McKinley, Superintendent Channel Islands National Park
11. Rebecca Jones Macko, Interpretive Park Ranger, Cuyahoga Valley National Park
12. Matthew Lamar, Park Ranger, Death Valley National Park
13. James Seale, Kennel Ranger, Denali National Park
14. Curtis Hall, Lead Ranger - Resource Education & Volunteers, Dry Tortugas National Park
15. Gabriel Curbelo, Administrative Program Specialist, Everglades National Park
16. Eric Tidwell, Visitor and Resource Protection Park Ranger, Gates of the Arctic National Park and Preserve
17. Pamela Sanfilippo, Museum Services & Interpretation Program Manager, Gateway Arch National Park
18. Karley Nugent, Park Guide, Glacier Bay National Park
19. Joëlle Baird, Lead Public Affairs Specialist, Grand Canyon National Park
20. Valerie Gohlke, Public Affairs Officer, Grand Teton National Park
21. Bradley Mills, Lead Astronomy Ranger, Great Basin National Park
22. Zack Brown, Park Guide, Great Sand Dunes National Park and Preserve
23. Theresa Moore, Acting Superintendent & Visitor Services Manager, Guadalupe Mountains National Park
24. Honeygirl Duman, Education Specialist & Hawaiian Community Liaison, Haleakalā National Park
25. Jessica Ferracane, Public Affairs Specialist, Hawai'i Volcanoes National Park
26. Ashley Waymouth, Interpretation Program Manager, Hot Springs National Park
27. Bill Smith, Park Guide, Indiana Dunes National Park
28. Liz Valencia, Interpretation and Cultural Resources Manager, Isle Royale National Park
29. Meg Rockwell, Park Guide, Joshua Tree National Park
30. Matt Johnson, Interpretation & Education Program Manager and Public Information Officer, Katmai National Park and Preserve
31. Jon Nicholson, Interpretation and Education Program Manager and Public Information Officer, Kobuk Valley National Park
32. Chelsea Niles, Program Manager for Interpretation, Education, & Partnerships, Lake Clark National Park & Preserve
33. Jim Richardson, Superintendent, Lassen Volcanic National Park
34. Molly Schroer, Management Analyst and Public Information Officer, Mammoth Cave National Park
35. Shannon Roberts, Education Program Coordinator, Mesa Verde National Park
36. Anthony Wyberski, Maintenance Supervisor, National Park of American Samoa

37. Eve West, Chief of Interpretation, New River Gorge National Park and Preserve
38. Yeva Cifor, Interpretive Park Ranger, North Cascades National Park Service Complex
39. Molly Pittman, Public Affairs Specialist, Olympic National Park
40. Amos Almy, Interpretive Park Ranger, Olympic National Park
41. Sarah Herve, Chief of Interpretation, Petrified Forest National Park
42. Rich Moorer, Supervisory Park Ranger, Pinnacles National Park
43. Serena Sinclair, Park Guide, Redwood National and State Parks
44. Jamie Richards, Public Affairs Specialist, Rocky Mountain National Park
45. Cam Juarez, Community Engagement & Outreach Coordinator and Public Information Officer, Saguaro National Park
46. Margo Roseum, Education Technician, Shenandoah National Park
47. Maureen McGee-Ballinger, Deputy Superintendent, Theodore Roosevelt National Park
48. Erik Ditzler, Senior Interpretive Specialist, Voyageurs National Park
49. Brian Powers, Interpretation Program Manager and Public Information Officer, White Sands National Park
50. Lydia Jones, Park Guide, Wind Cave National Park
51. Jamie Hart, South District Interpreter, Wrangell-St. Elias National Park and Preserve
52. Linda Veress, Public Affairs Specialist, Yellowstone National Park
53. Scott Gediman, Public Affairs Officer, Yosemite National Park
54. Jonathan Shafer, Public Affairs Specialist, Zion National Park
55. Steve T. Phan, Chief of Interpretation, Education & Visitor Services and Historic Weapons Supervisor, Camp Nelson National Monument
56. Chris Collins, Superintendent, New Philadelphia National Historic Site
57. Doug Mitchell, Executive Director, Glacier National Park Conservancy
58. Tigran Nahabedian, Instagram @jrrangertigran
59. Evan Wexler, Instagram @wexplorations
60. Patrick Rodden, Instagram @cliftonwanders
61. Cheyenne Yanez, Vic and Penny Robledo, Instagram @theadventurous3
62. Genevieve Lei, Instagram @gen_lei
63. Brad and Joy Ryan, Instagram @grandmajoysroadtrip
64. Mary Quan, Instagram @alohagirl_619
65. Kelsi Goss
66. Tavia Carlson, Instagram @bigbravenomad
67. Matt and Karen Smith, Instagram @mattandkarensmith
68. Amanda Bauler, Instagram @nationalparkfamilyquest
69. Sarah Olzawski
70. Chris Zayas, Instagram @chrisdixonz
71. Journey, Valerie, and Eric Castillo, Instagram @journey_castillo
72. Karen Aranda, Instagram @randomcairns
73. Kedar Halbe, Instagram @kedar.halbe
74. Corey Ford, Instagram @flightlevelfoto
75. Brandi Small, Instagram @brandihikes
76. Bobby Beaulieu, Instagram @mainerinrancho
77. Enza and Damian Vujicic, Instagram @enza_everywhere
78. Mick Dees, Instagram @nomad.mick
79. Andrew Fisher, Instagram @andrewfisher7
80. Bryan Dinello, Instagram @Sp1nell0
81. Christa Sellers, Instagram @christa.eileen
82. Pradeep Chandra, Instagram @inapcha
83. Karey J. Griffith, Instagram @thebuckethattraveler
84. Kathy Kupper, Public Affairs Specialist, National Park Service

▶ Image Credits

27 – Linda Mohammad
50-51 – Patrick Rodden
55 – Patrick Rodden
58 – Patrick Rodden
64 – Mike Bauler
65 – Patrick Rodden
66 – Patrick Rodden
73 – Patrick Rodden
77 – Tavia Carlson
78 – Patrick Rodden
83 – Andrew Fisher
85 – Patrick Rodden
87 – Mike Bauler
90 – Bradley Mills
112-113 – Christa Sellers
123 – Andrew Fisher
124 (top) – Valerie Golhke
124 (bottom) – Patrick Rodden
125 – Andrew Fisher
126-127 – Patrick Rodden
130 – Mike Bauler
131 – Andrew Fisher
133 – Andrew Fisher
140 – Peter Densmore
143 (top and bottom) – Patrick Rodden
147 (top) – Andrew Fisher
148 – Mike Bauler
154 – Andrew Fisher
155 – National Park Service

158-159 – Andrew Fisher
170-171 – Andrew Fisher
173 – Patrick Rodden
174 – Anderw Fisher
175 – Nick Lashley
176 – National Park Service
177 (top) – Andrew Fisher
178 (top) – National Park Service
179 – Mick Dees
182 – Laurence Parent
183 – Laurence Parent
186 – Patrick Rodden
190 – Patrick Rodden
192 – National Park Service
193 – Patrick Rodden
196 – Linda Mohammad
198-199 – Patrick Rodden
204 – Mick Dees
209 – Patrick Rodden
211 – Patrick Rodden
212 – Patrick Rodden
216 – Patrick Rodden
217 (top) – Patrick Rodden
217 (bottom) – Linda Mohammad
219 – Patrick Rodden
230 – Patrick Rodden
242-243 – Andrew Fisher
254-255 – Peter Densmore
All other images from Shutterstock

Grand Teton National Park
Wyoming

Acknowledgments

The best thing about living your bucket-list life is that you get to keep adding new things to the list. I checked off my bucket list to write a book on national parks when *The National Parks Bucket List* journal was first published, but to have the opportunity to sit down with park rangers from over 50 national parks across the country and almost two dozen national park lovers (many I have adventured with) and hear about their life stories and passion for our public lands is another level of bucket list item checked.

My gratitude goes to my team at Quarto: Lori for the incredible idea and trusting me to author this book, and my editor Katie, who is incredibly talented in reading my mind through my words, and helped me write concisely.

Words cannot describe my appreciation of the 84 contributors who made this collection of life stories and photography possible. To the park rangers across the US who made time to entertain my numerous emails and list of questions, thank you for allowing me into your worlds and for sharing anecdotes from your time on the job and the stories that led you to find your parks. To the park lovers across the globe, with various backgrounds and diverse perspectives, thank you for partaking in this meaningful journey. Your stories, captured by both words and photos, will inspire many others to explore our national parks. A very special hat tip to Ranger Kathy Kupper, the National Park Service's Public Affairs Specialist in Washington, DC, who made connections to all the park rangers across the 63 big parks.

This book wouldn't have been written in time without the unwavering support of my dear husband, Karey, who stayed up late through many nights to keep me company. Though there were fewer coffee runs this time around compared to the first book (due to the future Junior Ranger onboard), we did persevere.

To my National Park Geek family and The Bucket List Traveler community, thank you for being a part of my stories and many memories made at the parks. I would not have realized my American Dream without the friendship, camaraderie, and community we have fostered through the years.

And to you, reading this book and geeking out all over America's Best Idea, I truly appreciate you. May our paths cross someday on the trails or at the visitor centers.

Miles & Smiles,
Linda Mohammad

Sequoia National Park
California

Redwood National Park
California

About the Author

Linda Mohammad is a national park lover and self-proclaimed weekend warrior. Originally born and raised in Malaysia, she migrated to the United States in pursuit of her engineering degrees at Colorado School of Mines. Her passion for traveling stemmed from the good old college days, when she'd have to vacate her dorm room during school breaks. Her love for the national parks first sparked when she attended geology field trips as part of her school syllabus. Today, Linda is an engineer working in the energy industry, and California is her homebase. When she's not out visiting parks or solving engineering problems, Linda spends her time with clients as part of her life-coaching business, The Bucket List Life, where she helps people tap into their purpose and passion so they can live their bucket list life now. Known as The Bucket List Traveler on social media, she journals her way through the parks and documents her visits, and hiking, trip planning, storytelling, and list-making are her forte. On weekends, she can be found exploring some of our many national parks across the country. To date, she has checked off all 63 big national parks in the US and more than half of the 400+ national park units managed by the National Park Service. Follow her adventures at www.thebucketlisttraveler.com or on Instagram at @thebucketlisttraveler.

Bryce Canyon National Park
Utah